THE IDEAS BEHIND ALL

AINAN AHMAD

BLUEROSE PUBLISHERS
India | U.K.

Copyright © Ainan Ahmad 2023

All rights reserved by author. No part of this publication may be reproduced, stored in a retrieval system or transmitted in any form or by any means, electronic, mechanical, photocopying, recording or otherwise, without the prior permission of the author. Although every precaution has been taken to verify the accuracy of the information contained herein, the publisher assumes no responsibility for any errors or omissions. No liability is assumed for damages that may result from the use of information contained within.

BlueRose Publishers takes no responsibility for any damages, losses, or liabilities that may arise from the use or misuse of the information, products, or services provided in this publication.

For permissions requests or inquiries regarding this publication, please contact:

BLUEROSE PUBLISHERS
www.BlueRoseONE.com
info@bluerosepublishers.com
+91 8882 898 898
+4407342408967

ISBN: 978-93-5989-693-9

Cover design: Muskan Sachdeva
Typesetting: Pooja Sharma

First Edition: November 2023

….a collection of science, sexuality, gender, philosophy, humanities, education and business-related interests

Introduction

The Ideas behind All......a collection of science, sexuality, gender and philosophy-related interests is the 'nascence' of ideas associated with science, sexuality, gender and philosophy using familiar topical issues (titles) for each of them. It is a specificity of ideas that encompass the generality of the human concern. In a way, it is akin to the collection of journals or articles of varying interests

In this case, the ideas behind science, sexuality, gender and philosophy will be discussed under the sub-titles-*The Beyond-Physics Analogy of Newton's Laws of Motion, Understanding Heterosexual Dynamics Using Science, The Code-13 Principle (Sex Theory), Housewifery...giving the role of women a professional and an academic forte and Who Is Man?* With each h sub-title having its introductory/preface part /table of contents, chapters and will be followed by the next through pagination.

The Beyond-Physics Analogy of Newton's Laws of Motion explains beyond the three fundamental laws of motion in theory and by extension, it applications to advancement of countries, age-to- age civilizations and religious rituals e.g. prayers, using man as the analogous 'object' as case study in relation of realities as transcending the natural plane. Science in nature, it extends to the fields of philosophy (meta-physics), psychology and physics.

Understanding Heterosexual Dynamics Using Science seeks to use science in explaining the various forms of sexuality that exist between a man and woman before marriage, the emotional connections, sense of bonding and impact the audience with the analogous use of the scientific (magnetism and mechanics-based) principles with consequential psychological effects as they affect subsequent relationships(or marriages) individuals engage in. It makes use of novel terminologies to explain the various forms of sexual intercourse.

The Code-13 Principle (Sex Theory) is an article that puts to computation the number of times individuals, regardless of gender, had engaged in heterosexual intercourse before marriage, what they would likely face-in and out of relationships, how it would apply to sociology, sexology, psychology, and by extension, criminology-an approach to find criminals based on sexual behavioral tendencies.

Housewifery…giving the role of women a professional and an academic forte, a gender-based article or "journal", throws light on the possibility of making home-keeping (especially by women) a blend of academic and professional influence. It shows the road map as to how a stable society can arise by institutionalizing thepower of academics and professionalism in home-keeping and empowering women towards becoming good home-keepers.

Who Is Man? Is a philosophy or school of thought that asserts the descriptive "trinity" of man-man is a spirit, he has a soul and lives in a body. Using instances of buildings and the Soft drink, Coca Cola, it explains the 'vividness' of the philosophy.

*The Apparently Creeping Disappearance of Reading Culture In Modern Times*explains the rationale behind the seeming disappearance of book reading in the lives of people-children, juvenile, young adults and even the older ones.

*Business Success (The 7 'unavoidables' to succeeding in Business)*is a business interest that use the seven 'unavoidables' to explain the difference between successful business men and women and the unsuccessful ones-what makes nations greater than the other, from the business perspective.

F-R-I-E-N-D-S-H-P: The Meaning is a humanities interest that looks at the true FRIENDSHIP as the basis for long lasting relationships between and or amongst individuals-married and single and organizations. "It is in the acrostic, FRIENDSHIP", the article infers, "that determines how concrete a relationship existing between or amongst individuals and organizations."

Contents

Science: *The Beyond-Analogy of Newton's Laws of Motion* 1

    Introduction 2

    Chapter One: Newton's First Law Of Motion 4

    Chapter Two: Newton's Second Law Of Motion ... 9

    Chapter Three: Newton's Third Law of Motion ... 13

Sexuality: *(i) Understanding Heterosexual Dynamics Using Science* 16

    Preface 17

    Introduction 19

    Chapter One: The Case of 'No-Sexuality' Between Two Partners 21

    Chapter Two: The Case Of Higher Sexuality Between Two Partners 23

    Chapter Three: The Case Of 'Equal' Sexuality Between Two Partners 27

Sexuality: (II) *The Code 13 Principle(The Sex Theory)* .. 31

    Preface 32

    Introduction 35

    Chapter One: Analysis/ Derivation Of The Computable Equation 38

    Chapter Two: Interpretations, Impressions And Meaning Of Expressions Used 42

Chapter Three: Applications And Likely Future Projection..50

Gender: *Housewifery…giving the role of women a professional and an academic touch* 52

   Preface 53

   Introduction 57

   Chapter 1: Academic Housewifery 59

   Chapter 2: Professional Housewifery.....................65

Philosophy: *Who is Man?*..68

   Preface 69

   Introduction 71

   Chapter One: Man Is A Spirit..................................75

   Chapter Two: He Lives In A Body 80

   Chapter Three: He Has A Soul................................83

Education: *The Apparently Creeping Disappearance of Reading Culture In Modern Times*...................................88

   Preface 89

   Introduction 91

   Chapter One: Reason One..92

   Chapter Two: Reason Two 97

   Chapter Three: Reason Three 102

Business: *Business Success (The 7 'unavoidables' to succeeding in Business)* 108

   Preface 109

   Introduction 111

Chapter one: Defining the Orientation Of Business. 112

Chapter Two: Defining The Orientation Of Business. 116

Chapter Three: Knowledge Acquisition 120

Chapter Four: Keeping A Positive Attitude 126

Chapter Five: Taking Calculated Risks. 129

Chapter Six; Minimizing Losses And Maximizing Profits. 132

Chapter Seven: Taking Responsibility For Business Actions. 135

Chapter Eight: Being Investment Minded 137

Humanities: *F-R-I-E-N-D-S-H-I-P: The Meaning*......140

Introduction 142

F-R-I-E-N-D-S-H-I-P: The Meaning 142

Chapter One: Foundation 145

Chapter Two: Reliability 152

Chapter Three: Intimacy 155

Chapter Four: Encouragement 158

Chapter Five: 'Noticeablility' 162

Chapter Six: Dedication/Devotion 164

Chapter Seven: Support 167

Chapter Eight: Happiness 170

Chapter Nine: Information 173

Chapter Ten: Profundity 175

Science

The Beyond-Analogy of Newton's Laws of Motion

Introduction

The classical Newtonian laws of motion are very valid to this present day. As a matter of fact, the entirety of science has its uniqueness in the dynamic foundation of the laws of motion postulated by physicist, Sir Isaac Newton.

The 'Beyond-Physics' laws of motion is an analogy of their natural dynamics in the light of meta-physics. The only difference is in their units-presently, there are no fathomable yardsticks or measuring parameters to ascertain intrinsic (eternal) variables associated with this phenomenon (see their explanations in subsequent chapters)

The chapters are stated in the order of the laws of motion as well as subsequent 'beyond-physics' statements and analysis (explanations). Strictly, Newton's laws of motion focus on the action of forces, determining position and a direction of bodies acted on. Similarly, the 'beyond-physics' laws are influenced by a special force as the force of inspiration. While a body or an object is used to identify with Newton's laws of motion, man, humanity or mankind is the analogous body; used to identify with the 'beyond-physics' analogy of Newton's laws of motion...

The classical Newtonian laws of motion are very valid to this present day. As a matter of fact, the entirety of science has its uniqueness in the dynamic foundation of the laws of motion postulated by physicist, Sir Isaac Newton.

The 'Beyond-Physics' laws of motion is an analogy of their natural dynamics in the light of meta-physics. The only difference is in their units-presently, there are no fathomable yardsticks or measuring parameters to ascertain intrinsic (eternal) variables associated with this phenomenon (see their explanations in subsequent chapters)

The chapters are stated in the order of the laws of motion as well as subsequent 'beyond-physics' statements and analysis (explanations). Strictly, Newton's laws of motion focus on the action of forces, determining position and a direction of bodies acted on. Similarly, the 'beyond-physics' laws are influenced by a special force as the force of inspiration. While a body or an object is used to identify with Newton's laws of motion, man, humanity or mankind is the analogous body; used to identify with the 'beyond-physics' analogy of Newton's laws of motion…

Chapter One
Newton's First Law Of Motion

A body will continue to remain in a state of rest or exhibit a uniform motion on a straight line except acted on by an external force. In simple terms, a body will not move or be at a point on a plane until a force is acted on it. This is called the law of inertia. Inertia is the state of a body to exhibit reluctance to stop when it moving or reluctance to move when it stops moving.

Below are diagrams showing

a) When a body (stone, say,) is not acted on by a force (in terms of positioning)

b) When the stone is finally acted on by a force (in terms of positioning)

a) Here, the stone is positioned at Ao on a road without being pushed or kicked against (acted on by external forces). Consequently, the stone will be unmoved or remain static, even to the end of time, provided there are no forces (kicking or pushing) acting on it.

Fig 1

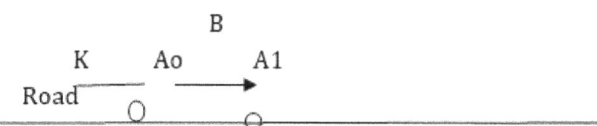

Fig 2

The stone is kicked against by an external force from its initial position at Ao to point A1. B shows the observed path or direction from Ao to A1 (where k is the applied force).

Akin to the first law of motion, the first 'beyond-physics' law is stated as

1) Man will continue to remain unchanged (or in analogous state of rest) except acted by an external force of change (usually in the form of thoughts). This may be referred to as the law of inertia of man.

In this case, the term of 'inertia' refers to the reluctance of or difficulty experienced by man to change his thought process when used to the already familiar ones. Better yet, it is a state of man getting stuck to what he is familiar with; refusing shift of thoughts or experiencing daunting challenges to accept change. Also, it refers to the reluctance of mankind to halt new changes as it embraces them.

The diagrams below explain succinctly this law

a) Fig 3

This shows the unmoved position of man (m) in the radar path of time at a particular period T. If there is no change in his thought process (force of thought), despite time progress, B1 and B2,(arbitrary) he will continue to remain at T; getting stuck or mentally refusing to move with time.

The Dark Age period in Europe is a typical illustration of this fact. The reason this age experienced limited progress or strictly, theoretically no development was because the Law of Inertia of Man was at work in them- the people of this time were so stuck in medieval thoughts of the medieval times (T) that appreciating available technologies in terms of advancement was a daunting task. Afterall, a change in the thought process of the people would have led to a better appreciation of available technologies. However, the reverse was the case. Hence, the name Dark Age; a period where no significant progress was made, not primarily due to limited available facilities, but a stuck-in-thought minds of the people not to appreciate the time and space they found themselves-holding onto familiarized values or finding difficult acceptance of mental shift to commensurate with the changing times (the mental inertia of the Dark Age people to external forces of change of thoughts).

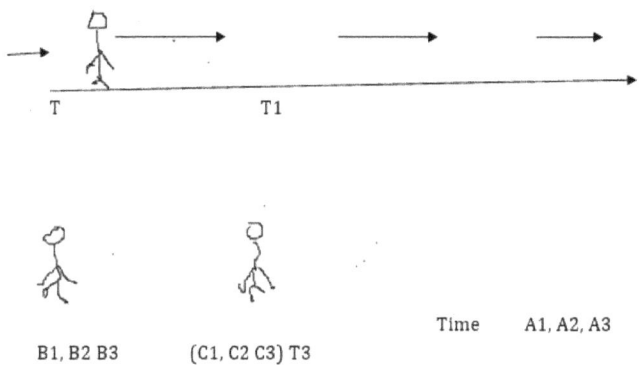

The diagram shows the forces (as indicated by arrows) as being responsible for the change in man's mentality at times T T1 and T3 with progressions (or developments) A1, A2 A3 to C1, C2 C3 (and even to the very end of time, including the last of humanity-man!); a result of the actions of forces of change.

An example of this application is the continued trend of development progress from the Dark Ages to our contemporary era, to the time of earthly ending. The forces of change (forces of inspiration) have brought about a change in the thought of process of man, engendering better and more advanced humanity (as shown by objects) and steady developments or progress (ions); A1, A2 A3, B1, B2, B3, C1, C2, C3 and so on to the progress made at the 'last phase of humanity' –epitomizing the earth's ending. The developments could be in the forms of social, political scientific and technological breakthroughs (in the positives or negatives) man has attained through those times.

There have been significant changes in the ages of man's existence; from the Dark Ages to our era, and even to the coming ages. Obviously, this is as a result of the action of the forces of change through the ages. Compare the situation with Fig 2.

(Note: All diagrams are not drawn to scale)

What complexion will things presently take if the inertia of man had persisted after the Dark Age?

Chapter Two

Newton's Second Law Of Motion

The force applied on a body is proportional to the change rate in momentum. Mathematically,

FαMo/t, where Mo=Momentum of the particle

F=Applied Force

t=time

Since Momentum=Velocity change * Mass

Therefore, Mo=ΔV/T* Mass (m)

Where ΔV=V-U, i.e. V =Final velocity, U=Initial velocity

Hence, Mo= (V-U)* M

FαMo

F=K* Mo, where $\overrightarrow{K}$=proportionality constant=1

Therefore, F=KM (V-U)/t=M (V-U)/t

Now, we will state the second 'beyond-physics' law of motion this way:

The force of inspiration propels man beyond the limited pinnacle of the earth's dimension-time and space to the destinations of realms beyond physical reach and is proportional to the product (outcome) of what is contained in man (an analogous statement of the quantity of matter or mass of an object)-quality of information, revelation, awareness level, consciousness and receptiveness change in relation to eternity. In a mathematical format,

FIαMi*ΔVi/Eα

Fi=Force of inspiration on man

Mi=Quality or quantity of information man contains, degree of revelational understanding of the realms propelled to and consciousness level

ΔVi = Change in receptiveness

Eα=Eternity

For ΔVi, in comparison with ΔV=V-U, we have ΔVi= Vi-Ui

Where Vi = peak of receptiveness to revelations or information received at the realms propelled to, Ui=Threshold and peak receptiveness of information at the various three-dimensional spheres of the earth.

At the various realms greater than the earth's time and space axis, time no longer exist. Rather, a 'timeless' recognition known as eternity takes the place of earthly time.

FIαMi*ΔVi/Eα

F=K*Mi*ΔVi/Eα= K*Mi (Vi-Ui)/Eα

Where K=Constant of proportionality (Constant of universality) =Change=1

The only true constant in all dynamics of man, nature and beyond the earth is 1; a statement of certainty.

Hence, $F_i = M_i (V_i - U_i)/E\alpha$

Notice that while the natural force is measured in Newton (N) or Kilogram Meter per Second square (Kgm/s2), initial and final velocities in Meter per Second (M/S), time in Second (S), Mass in Kilograms (K) and Momentum, a product of mass and velocity, measured in Kilograms Second(KgS), the parameters used to mathematically analyze the 'beyond-physics' second law of motion are immeasurable-they are all eternal-they transcend physical measurement. Moreover, it is impossible to compute these parameters. It is like dividing a number by infinity! There is no significant physical outcome (an approximated or near-zero value reached). Nonetheless, there is or are great significance attained by this 'physically awkward arithmetic' taking place beyond the physical plane.

This accounts for the varying degrees of technological socio-political cultural and economic advancements that distinctly separate nations through the ages of man's existence. The force of inspiration propels man from the threshold or peak of the limited earth's space and time dimension or level of accepted standards (appreciation, recognition and use of knowledge gained by experience and reasoning within the walls of the earthly realm) to the destinations of realms of greater advantages.

Based on man's receptiveness to comprehend revelation-based information on the grounds of consciousness, a key recognition is brought to the world and in no time, becomes and forms a constituent of advancement of nations and an explanation as to why countries are distinct in their affairs (peculiar practices of socio-political, cultural, scientific, technological and economic dictates).

Chapter Three

Newton's Third Law of Motion

Forces of action and reaction are equal and opposite. In other words, for every action there is an equal but opposite reaction. This is applicable in the principle or law of equilibrium.

When a body is placed on a support, the body exerts its weight on it. But in order to balance the force due to the weight of the body, the support provides a reaction to ensure stability.

The diagram below shows the weight of a steel strip placed on a wooden bench.

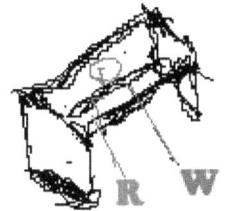

Fig. 5 Not Drawn to scale

The steel strip (the zero-like red label) exerts its weight (W) on the wooden bench (see diagram above). To ensure stability or balance, the steel strip creates a reaction (R), a product of resistance of its four-member support.

Therefore, an analogous third 'beyond-physics' law of motion is stated as:

For every transcending force of inspiration, there is an equal but opposite transcending response (reaction). Since the force of inspiration transcends space-time dimension, we will give a comparative perspective to explain this 'special fact'. This is the law of balance.

When a body known as the human mind is placed on an equal support of meditation, the weight of the mind's visualizations or captured pictures of envisaged happenings is balanced by a corresponding reaction; a product of deep thoughts (muttering, focus and intense cogitations) is created to bring about a mutual harmony.

However, due to the limited space-time dimension, immediate manifestations cannot be seen. Just as how long it takes a large volume water to pass through a very narrowly open path, so it is for a large 'volume' or magnitude of the harmony or concordance between the mind's visualizations and corresponding deep thoughts from eternity to pass through or come to pass in the physical. This is due to a very structured narrow or restricted path of the earth's space and time.

In the religious circles, some prayer-conscious individuals wonder why there are no instant answers to their prayers. In fact, it appears their prayers are falling into the 'deaf ears' of their Creator. Conversely, this is because the 'large' magnitude of the mind's visualization as engineered by the individual's prayers and corresponding anticipations in the form of deep thoughts reaching a harmony in the light of manifestation from eternity is restricted owing to the restricted time and space of the earth.

In all, the depth of information can best be appreciated only if man Meta-physically Ascend Naturally. The ability to stretch his natural limits and see them as attentiveness mechanisms to the realms of understanding, despite inhabiting in the natural will be of utmost importance to have a complete grasp of the write-up.

Sexuality

(i) Understanding Heterosexual Dynamics Using Science

Preface

The application of science in many fields of human endeavors is undoubtedly not far-fetched. As a matter of fact, science has profound applications on human behaviors, especially sexuality. Sexuality, an integral form of human behavior, can be explained using science. Precisely, science can be explained in the light of heterosexuality in the context of this literary piece.

Understanding Heterosexual Dynamics Using Science explains the various forms of sexuality that exist between a man and woman before marriage, the emotional connections, sense of bonding and impact the audience with the analogous use of the scientific (magnetism and mechanics-based) principles with consequential psychological effects as they affect subsequent relationships(or marriages) individuals engage in. It makes use of novel terminologies to explain the various forms of sexual intercourse. With the use of diagrams, the creativity understanding of the reader-worthy work piece intends reaching the bull's eye.

It is intended that the reader comprehend this sexuality-based material and appreciate its essence in relationships with the opposite sex. In addition, this brief masterpiece will essentially be useful by sexologists, scientists and other academicians interested in the subject matter.

Understanding Heterosexual Dynamics Using Science merits consideration amongst scholars, students of sexology, psychology and the general reading public.

Ainan Ahmad

Introduction

Science, an organized body of knowledge, is applicable in sexuality-related matters-heterosexuality. Precisely, Understanding Heterosexual Dynamics Using Science applies fundamental scientific principles such as law of magnetism and mechanics (momentum) to explain the consequences of the various sexual dynamics.

The sexual dynamics as mentioned in the table of contents section of this literary piece simply refers to the various kinds of sexual intercourse involving individuals of the opposite sex and their consequences as they affect the mental and social definitions of subsequent relationships they may involve themselves in. In the heterosexual sense, it demystifies the 'mysteries' that have to do with the various sexual dynamics between a man and woman; unveiling aftermaths of their 'presence'.

The chapters are expatiated using diagrams, succinct situations and a great deal of scientific approach mechanisms to bringing to the easy comprehension of readers the powers behind the various sexual dynamics as they affect relationships and marriages. As a novel piece, the author has put together an array of terminologies of scientific background and their meanings for readers to peruse and grasp for easy follow-ups. The Table of Contents section reveals chapters (titles), terminologies and meanings and author's bibliography makes this work-piece a reading delight.

Students, researchers, teachers and other concerned professionalsand academics will find this piece understandable. It is the hope of the writer that readers find this useful to help better their union with their spouses from a heterosexual perspective.

Chapter One

The Case of 'No-Sexuality' Between Two Partners

One of the fundamental principles of magnetism recognizes the fact that like poles repels and unlike poles attract. We would say it is akin to this case. However, it is really the other way round. In other words, as regards sexuality, like poles (partners with 'no-sexuality' status) attracts and unlike poles (Partners with 'equal' sexuality status as we will see in Chapter Three) repel. The difference?

Let us consider what takes place between two particles A and B before and after collision as shown in the diagram below. Here, A and B possess the same weightless constituents.

A ———————→   ←——————— B

Before Collision

NOT DRWAN TO SCALE

A ——————————— B

After Collision

The diagrams show the state of particles A and B before and after collision. Similarly, this is what happens when two 'no-sexuality' attached couples come together in a relationship or marriage. We can see that after collision, there is an intersection of the two particles. They are theoretically inseparable.

Consequently, such a relationship is free from the distrust, insecurity, doubts and uncertainties as togetherness (a strong sense of oneness of personality) and conspicuous sexual compatibility abound.

Granted, in a heterosexual sense, like the fundamental principle of magnetism, a man is generally attracted to a woman. However, *it is in the place of those who practically understand the value of 'no-sexuality' to know that the happiest marriage exists when a man who has maintained a 'no-sexuality' status marries a woman of his kind.*

Chapter Two

The Case Of Higher Sexuality
Between Two Partners

What happens when a partner's level of sexuality is higher than his or her spouse? In this chapter, we will view it from a scientific point of view and relate it in a way as it affects relationships and marriages of people. This is a two-case scenario:

1) When a man's sexuality is higher than that of his spouse

2) When a woman's sexuality is higher than that of her spouse.

<u>Scientific viewpoint</u>: We have read, been taught, studied and practically observed that when a body (A, say) of a greater momentum collides with a small body (b, say), the collision after-math will be that both bodies will move with a common velocity (the velocity moved by the body possessing greater momentum). The diagrams below bare them all.

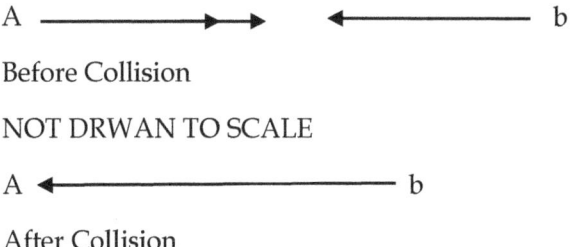

A ——————▶   ◀—————— b

Before Collision

NOT DRWAN TO SCALE

A ◀—————————— b

After Collision

It can be said that the both particles will be moving with a common velocity due to the overriding influence of A (Possession of a greater momentum). With this analogy, let us look into the two –case scenario we earlier mentioned.

1) <u>When a man's sexuality is higher than that of his spouse</u>

This implies that the man, the analogous body A, possessor of a greater momentum, sexually has an influence over his spouse. In other words, the 'common velocity' of eventual heterosexuality between them will be in the direction of the man's sexual influence.

Of course, there are implications. A man's experience of heterosexual relations over his spouse will undoubtedly create imbalances in the sincerity of relationships between them. For instance, a man who has seen it all when it comes to sexual matters of this kind will very likely seek for pleasure outside the bounds of his union, especially when she is naïve in her sexual interactions with him. On the part of the woman, if logic is applied, she will be made to realize that there are likely uncertainties in his being faithful to her because he is linked to other partners he had had sexual relations with. Obliterating the veils of deception and pseudo-love, these discrepancies surface.

2) When a Woman's Sexuality is Higher Than That of Her Spouse

Similar to Case 1, the woman is the analogous body whose momentum is greater than that of the man. And as such, excluding hypocrisy and other 'put-ups' by the woman in communicating sexuality to him, the woman pose a huge influence in the sexual affairs with her spouse. The eventual heterosexual dynamic between the man and woman will have a common velocity influenced by the woman.

Just as what happens when a man's sexuality is greater than that of his spouse, a man's rationale will raise a lot of questions; her direct relationships with her partners over the years, her fidelity and being trustworthy. What might be baffling will be that his being gratified is as a result of the product of experiences gained by interacting sexually with other people over the years. To the extreme, if not meticulously looked into, such a situation leads to separation between both parties and worse still, divorce.

No wonder people marry for trivial reasons (such as higher degree sexual competence) and as a result, divorce as a result of trivial reasons (such as suspicion of infidelity, distrust and other uncertainties). It is seldom advised that individuals should not involve themselves in relationships leading to marriages with people who are more experienced than they to avoid irregularities like those. In addition, it is said that people who had engaged in sexual intercourses in time past are at least, twice as likely to indulge in extra-marital affairs. Like an unchecked habit picked from childhood, people with this sexual orientation find it difficult to halt it.

In all, this is an underlying fact: *The sexual relations a man or woman had had in time past with his or her partners (he or she will be bonded or soul-tied to them emotionally) will for the rest of his or her life, irrespective of the union he or she is involved in, color and more importantly, pose a profound secondary influence in his or her present and/or subsequent relations.*

Chapter Three

The Case Of 'Equal' Sexuality Between Two Partners

As earlier stated, we know that the law of magnetism recognize like poles repel and unlike poles attract. It is applicable here. As the subject matter suggests, the like poles refer to the equal sexuality that exist between two partners involved in a heterosexual relationship.

In the convince of this issue, what becomes the heterosexual relationship between a habitual gigolo and a prostitute?

Now, what happens when two bodies of equal amount of momentum collide? The diagrams below shows what becomes of them. Consider the bodies A and B.

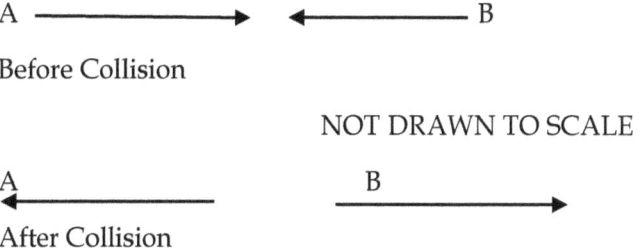

Obviously, it can be said that after collision both bodies, A and B drifted apart from each other owing to the equal amount of momentum they have. In the same vein, it becomes the aftermath of individuals whose sexuality is theoretically the same.

Like the old saying:' no two captains can be in a ship', there are no two partners that practically possess equal sexuality-one must be ahead of the other-either the man ahead of the woman (vice versa). *Else, incompatibility will be dominant. Simply, the demonstration of equal sexuality between both partners will in no time engender di-vision, owing to observed 'struggle for sexual dominance' and eventually leads to marital divorce and break-ups in relationships. Akin to an in-born habit, the partners, as a matter of gratifying their insatiable sexual needs, will, with or without their individual consent seek for pleasure outside the limits of the union.*

Scientific Terminologies and Their Meanings in Heterosexual Dynamics

1) <u>Momentum:</u> In scientific mechanics, momentum is defined as the product of the mass of a body and velocity. Now, we all know that velocity is simply the distance (displacement) per unit time. Therefore, momentum, as used in heterosexual dynamics, is simply the experience ('weights' or 'deposits') of sexuality gained by the individual with various partners (from one to the other) over the years. It can be represented using the format below

Momentum= Mass*Velocity≡ Bonding between the individual and those whom he or she had had sexual relations with.

2) <u>Particles:</u> In science, particles simply refer to weightless object. Similarly, the word 'particle' is used to describe those who have not gained momentum; have not been bonded to people by virtue of sexual relations.

3) <u>Collision:</u> The term 'collision' refers to the deliberate or sudden coming together of bodies. In analogy, Collision, in Heterosexual dynamics, refers to the coming together of individuals into unions; especially relationships leading to marriage.

4) <u>Common Velocity:</u> In a strict scientific recognition, common velocity is the velocity reached after the collision involving a body with greater momentum and another with a smaller body. Usually, it is the body with a greater momentum that collides with the less-momentum body. Akin to this recognition, common velocity is the eventual influence used by a partner whose momentum or bonding is more superior or stronger than his or her spouse in heterosexual relations with each other.

5) <u>Bodies:</u> It is simply referring to objects with measurable mass or weights. In the same vein, it is a word used in describing those who,

irrespective of momentum difference, have acquired some experience heterosexual relations.

6) <u>Like Poles and Unlike Poles:</u> In magnetism, like poles refer to points on a magnet that repel each other. Unlike Poles refer to points on a magnet that attract each other. In a typical contradicting heterosexual sense, unlike poles as read in chapters two and three, are simply those whose sexuality cannot be truly incompatible and like poles, as read in chapter one is just the exact opposite.

Sexuality

(II) The Code 13 Principle

(The Sex Theory)

Preface

If you are married and reading this, a question (awkward it may seem) would have to be asked: 'Before marriage, how many times have you had sex?" Do not trivialize this as it would be very necessary.

Probably, you are looking with disdain! It is understandable. As a matter of fact; if you use this question to X-ray different people on the streets, living in a district or community, you will be amazed at the various responses you would get. Some will give questionable numerical figures (taking the question with levity), others will not answer you, believing that you want to infringe on their privacy. Funny enough, other individuals would say something like 'I will tell you later' while others will respond by unleashing life-threatening words and actions on you.

However, if sex is an experience, should it be an off-the-record account, worth remembering and documenting, kept as secret for a time but (think about this question: is anything hidden under the sun?) or something to remembered when you are in the grave!?

If it is an off-the –record account, then why waste your time on a task you will not commend of yourself of doing, after all, anything worth doing is worth doing well?

If it is worth remembering and documenting, then you should be congratulated!

This is because you are about exercising empirical knowledge to others (interested), letting them (the wise ones) learn what are ordinarily vague when taught and possibly help improve the sex life of others before and after the particular time (marriage).

If you are advocating that it should be kept secret for a time, think of the question asked. Do you know that the wall has ears? One way or the other, the other party you had it with will unravel to his or her world what really happened. In time, this could be implicating.

If you are that individual who sees the experience, sex, as something to be remembered when you are in the grave, what an exclamation it is. Remember, it is just one life you and I have to live.

If you portray this disposition, it means that you are in a state of guilt. Imagine you carrying this burden of guilt all your life. How miserable you would be! No one you could share it with?

Then, you are out of this world! Frankly, you are in a world of your own.

How can an individual best know the actual number of times he or she had had sex before marriage?

'Record keeping of sex activities helps to ascertain one's level of sexuality and in a way, behavioral disposition, present and in future'…Ainan Ahmad

Introduction

The Code-13 Principle ' is a write-up, taking to cognizance a postulation that computes the number of times individuals had engage in sexual intercourse before marriage using a theoretical mechanism known as the computable equation. Here, sexual intercourse refers to the direct relationship or contact between a man and woman.

The Code-13 Principle (The Sex Theory) computes from the first-sex experience to the point just before the nuptial knots were tied. The work piece takes to consideration certain parameters, conditions and has several interpretations, signs and symbols. In practical terms, the interpretations that form the computable equation are impressionistic assertions by the author.

Interestingly, the computable equation has thirteen interpretations. These interpretations give the various sex lives of individuals ranging from the simple to complex; resulting in various impressions by the author.

It is said that 'there is no smoke without fire'. Therefore, the genesis behind the ageless phenomenon undoubtedly needs to be unveiled. It is titled 'come to think of it, sex!'

Come To Think Of It, Sex!(An Overview)

The book, titled Come To Think Of It, Sex! Is a driven_ by_ inspiration interest which focuses on the true qualities of sex as the basis for its definition. It is pleasure _ filled, somewhat funny but possesses didactic remarks on the appropriation of sex.

It is a mini-sized young adult-based book that has in its identity creatively designed chapters that give the reader not only a sense of appreciation but the urge to 'thirst' for more.

The chapters in this book are designed such that they complemented each other. How?

The juxtaposition of the God-factor as the originator of the issue, sex, with the worldly influence on it (as we progress) is obviously stated.

Simply, Come To Think Of It Sex! Creatively puts to computation (arithmetic calculation) the sex life of different individuals, asserts the factor responsible for sex and explains its "inevitables". Based on the computation, it extrapolates the future of the mentioned sex-performing individuals, all other things being equal, when the institution, marriage, knocks on their doors knocks on their doors. Its three-chapter conceptualization is brought about by creatively giving the term SEX an acrostic, that is,

S-Simply

E-Erotic

X-Xperience

(Where 'X' takes the pronunciation of 'Ex' as in Experience)

In other words, the word SEX, according to this write-up, has three qualities-Simplicity, Eroticism and Experience. Put simply, sex is simple by nature, erotic by feel and an experience as an activity (especially when viewed in the light of sexual intercourse).

On these premises, Come To Think Of It, Sex! has its three chapter uniqueness spelt out as Simplicity (Simply), Eroticism (Erotic) and Experience (Xperience) and as Chapter 1, 2 and 3.

Simplicity: Chapter 1 explains the creative or acrostic identification of the male and female sex organs as 'major devices' for action

Eroticism: Chapter 2 explains the factor responsible for the interaction or action of the creatively asserted male and female sex organs. In simple terms, Chapter 2 is a complement of Chapter 1

Experience: The coming together of Chapters 1 and 2 give what is contained in Chapter 3. Chapter 3 takes to account the number of times individuals, irrespective of gender, had engaged in sexual intercourse before marriage…

The Code-13 Principle (The Sex Theory) is a detailed expression of the experience quality of sex (of the title, Come To Think Of It, Sex!).

Note: It is the desire of the writer that this work-piece be termed 'The Code-13 Principle', whence accepted.

Chapter One
Analysis/ Derivation Of The Computable Equation

As stated, the computable equation takes to account the first-sex experience to the point before the nuptial knots were tied (marriage).

We begin by using a case study -individual A. Individual A, a model, is a representative of the male and female gender-it could be a 'he' or 'she'. Below is an arithmetic computation of the number of time the individual A had had sex. Let us establish the following parameters.

a. Let the first time individual A had sex. (with partner, a, say) be X

b. Let the subsequent number of times individual A had had sex be X1, (with the same partner)

c. Perhaps there is an eventual break-up, let number of times individual a had engaged in sex in subsequent relationships with the partners (b, c, d, e… say,) be X2,

d. Considering the number of times individual A had had for_the moment/one-night-stand sex, with partners (f, g, h, l,….)., If individual A had engaged in such, let the number of times individual A had engaged in one-night-stand/

for_ the_ moment sex be X3 (with partners f, g,h, l...) (On basis of assumption).

e. Assuming individual A 'hooks up' with a would-be life-long marriage material (partners Z, say) let the number of times individual A had sexually engaged partners Z be X4. This is before marriage

f. Considering the parameters, we can compute (arithmetically) the numbers of times individual A had engaged in sex before marriage. Let the numbers of times individual A engaged in sex be represented by n. therefore, it follows that: $n = X \pm X1 \pm X2 \pm X3 \pm X4$. In other words, the number of times individual A had engaged in sex can be given as: the first time individual A had sex (with partner a, say) ± the subsequent number of times individual A had sex with the same partner ± the number of times individual A had engaged in subsequent relationships

(with partners b, c, d, e..., say,) ± The Number of times individual A had engaged in a one-night-stand/ for the moment sex (with partners f, g, h, I, ...) ± Number of times individual A had engaged in sex with partners Z (the would- be - lifelong marriage material).

For convenience, let us represent the following

a. n by N (Number of times)

b. X by No (with partner A)

c. X1 by N1 (with the same partner)

d. X2 by N2 (with partners b, c, d, e…)

e. X3 by N3 (with partners f, g, h, I …)

f. X4 by N4 (with partners Z)

Therefore, n= X ± X1 ± X2 ± X3 ± X4 becomes N= No ± N1 N2 ± N3 ± N4. This is called the computable equation or the postulation's mechanism. Also, it is the generalized equation that summarizes the various sex lives of different individuals, ranging from the simple to the complex (as stated in the introductory part of this write-up).

The generalized equation or computable equation has thirteen mathematical interpretations. In other words, the equation, expressed as N= No ± N1 N2 ± N3 ± N4 can be interpreted as:

1) N=No+N1+N2+N3+N4…(Interpretation1)

2) N=No+N1+N2+N3…(Interpretation 2)

3) N=No+N1+N2…(Interpretation3)

4) N=No+N1+N3…(Interpretation 4)

5) N=No+N1+N4…(Interpretation 5)

6) N=No+N2+N4…(Interpretation 6)

7) N=No+N3+N4…(Interpretation 7)

8) N=No+N2+N3…(Interpretation 8)

9) N=No+N1…(Interpretation 9)

10) N=No+N2…(Interpretation 10)

11) N=No+N3…(Interpretation 11)

12) N=No+N4…(Interpretation 12)

13) N=No… (Interpretation 13).

Chapter Two
Interpretations, Impressions and Meaning Of Expressions Used

At this point, a number of questions are expected to be asked. The parameters, signs and other intricacies that form the postulation's mechanism (the computable equation) are major perspectives where questions are asked.

Interestingly, the validity or authenticity of the postulation is based on three statements:

1) The validity of the equation is partly dependent on relationships engaged. Usually, relationships as used in this context are sex-linked.

2) There is always a constant (that is, first-sex experience number) of 1

3) The computable equation will be valid provided the sincerity of the individual (individual A, in this case) in terms of record keeping of his or her sex activities; number of times of engaged sexual intercourse is taken to account.

These statements are related to each other and give the postulation's mechanism its standing uniqueness. Therefore, to appreciate the factors necessary for the uniqueness of the computable equation, vivid explanations have to be made.

(1): The Write-up considers sex in the light of sexual intercourse; the active involvement of a man and woman in direct physical contact with each other. Therefore, the computable equation takes to cognizance the number of partners individual A had engaged in sexual intercourse before marriage (a, b, c, d, e...z)

(2): The thirteen mathematical interpretations have a constant value of 1, irrespective of sex life; simple or complex because there is a first-sex experience number-No. Hence, the computable equation $N = N_o \pm N_1 \, N_2 \pm N_3 \pm N_4$ becomes $N = 1 \pm N_1 \, N_2 \pm N_3 \pm N_4$ and the following mathematical interpretations

1 $N = N_o + N_1 + N_2 + N_3 + N_4$

2 $N = N_o + N_1 + N_1 + N_3$

3 $N = N_o + N_1 + N_2$

4 $N = N_o + N_1 + N_3$

5 $N = N_o + N_2 + N_3$

6 $N = N_o + N_1 + N_4$

7 $N = N_o + N_3 + N_4$

8 $N = N_o + N_2 + N_4$

9 $N = N_o + N_1$

10 $N = N_o + N_2$

11 $N = N_o + N_3$

12 $N = N_0 + N_4$

13 $N = N_0$

Now becomes

1 $N = 1 + N_1 + N_2 + N_3 + N_4$

2 $N = 1 + N_1 + N_2 + N_3$

3 $N = 1 + N_1 + N_2$

4 $N = 1 + N_1 + N_3$

5 $N = 1 + N_2 + N_3$

6 $N = 1 + N_1 + N_4$

7 $N = 1 + N_3 + N_4$

8 $N = 1 + N_2 + N_4$

9 $N = 1 + N_1$

10 $N = 1 + N_2$

11 $N = 1 + N_3$

12 $N = 1 + N_4$

13 $N = 1$

(3): The validity of the computable equation is dependent on the sincerity of the individual in terms of keeping records of his or her activities of sexual intercourse with partners he or she engages with.

However, from feasibility studies, there are questionable (as a matter of fact, there are no sincerity-given) answers as regards the number of individuals have engaged in sexual intercourse before marriage (Read the preface).

Nonetheless, the work piece uses a hypothetical approach of the model, individual A as case study to assert the number of times he or she (might) have engaged in sex before calling singlehood quits with partners (a, b, c, d, e, f…k, m, n,…z).Note: The partners stated are based on the conjecture of the writer regarding the number of partners individual A should have engaged in sexual intercourse before marriage.

A Typical Hypothetical Instance

We take mathematical interpretation (1) as case study for a sex-life situation of individual A;

$N=N_o+N_1+N_2+N_2+N_3+N_4$

A) Of course, the first-sex number is constant-with partner a. Therefore, $N_o=1$. Subsequently, let the number of times individual A had engaged in sex with the same partner be α. Hence, $N_1=\alpha$

B) There was an eventual demise. In this case, we tae as case studies sexual interactions between individual A and the following partners

(I) b (ii) c (iii) d (IV) e (v) f

Let the number of times individual A had engaged partner b be θ

Also, let the number of times individual A engaged partner c be W

We represent the number of times individual A had engaged partner d by ŭ

Let the number of times sexual intercourse existed between individual A and partner e be ë

Let the number of times sexual intercourse experienced between individual A and partner f be ẅ

Therefore $N2 = θ + W + ŭ + ë + ẅ$

C) Obviously, there were sexual interactions between individual A and the following partners (in this case, we take partners I, j, k, m, and n as case studies); one-night sex event

(1) i (2) j (3) k (4) m (5) n

Let the number of times individual A had engage in sexual intercourse with partner I be A

Also, we represent the number of times individual A and partner j had experienced sex together be B

Let the number of times sex experienced between individual A and partner k be C

Let the number of times sex existed between individual A and partner m be D

We represent the number of times individual A had engaged partner n in sex be E

Hence, $N3 = A + B + C + D + E$

D) Taking to consideration the number of times individual A had engaged in sexual intercourse with partner z; his or her life-partner (just before marriage), let the number of times sex existed between them be F. Therefore, N4=F

Based on these hypothetical analysis, the equation N=No+N1+N2+N3+N4 becomes N=1+ α+ (θ+ W+ ǔ+ ë+ ẅ) + (A+B+C+D+E) +F

Impressions

Sometimes referred to as impressionistic viewpoints, the writer 'assigns labels' to individuals whose sex lives fall under the various categories or interpretations of the generalized equation.

As asserted, there are two various sex lives of individuals; simple and complex sex lives. The impressions or labels given to the simple and complex sex lives are borne out of the author's judgment and are subject to debate.

Typically, interpretations (1) and (13) are examples of simple and complex sex lives exhibited by various individuals. Between them lies an array of interpretations of individuals whose sex lives are depicting varying degrees of complexity and simplicity.

The basis for the simple and complex sex lives is the kind of partners engaged. For instance, an individual whose sex life is interpreted as the equation N=No+N1+N2+N3+N4 is said to be living a complex sex life because he or she had engaged (before marriage) partners (b, c, d, e. f…I, j,k, m, n) before meeting or settling down with partner z. In other words, N2 and N3 parameters; implying that

$N = N_o + N_1 + N_2 + N_3 + N_4$ is the most complex.

Between (1) and (13) are exhibited levels of complexity and simplicity. The presence of N4 is theoretically a 'halting factor', acting as a full stop- absenting N2 and N3. For instance, the equations $N = N_o + N_2$,

$N = N_o + N_1 + N_2$, $N = N_o + N_3$, $N = N_o + N_1 + N_3$ and $N = N_o + N_2 + N_3$ indicate an orderly up-rise in the complex sex lives of individuals (due to increased number of partners and more importantly, presence of the parameters N2 and N3). Equations $N = N_o + N_1$ and $N = N_o$ indicate a down-rise in the simple sex lives of individuals. However, the stated equations depict individuals whose sex lives are still in the making except for the inclusion of the parameters N4 (They are subject to change at any time). Meanwhile, before embracing the 'halting factor', N4, individuals, whose sex lives had the elements N2 and N3 were indifferent form those whose sex lives currently possess them.

$N = N_o + N_1 + N_2 + N_3 + N_4$ shows the sex life lived by a prostitute, perhaps a nymphomaniac, nymphomaniac or simply, a sex addict. $N = N_o$ depicts the sex life of a celibate or secondary virgin. The equations between (1) and (13) show the sex lives of individuals as 'hierarchical agents' of promiscuity, infidelity, labeled sluts, sex maniacs or whores of the present day.

Meaning of Expressions Used

The generalized equation $N = N_o \pm N_1 \pm N_2 \pm N_3 \pm N_4$ has two conspicuous signs-the plus and minus. What are they? What do they imply?

a) The Plus sign: The plus sign denotes 'in agreement with' or 'agrees with'. Precisely, it is the agreement with or inclusion of other parameters of the given equation. If there are variables N_2 and N_3 in the equation $N = N_o + N_2 + N_3$, say, it is said that individual A's sex life is in agreement with $N = N_o + N_2 + N_3$. $N = N_o + N_1 + N_2 + N_3$ is an equation establishing a fact- individual A's sex life agrees with the presence of the elements N_1, N_2 and N_3. It is denoted by +.

b) The Minus sign: The minus sign denotes 'not in agreement with' or 'not agrees with'. It is the exclusion or not-in-agreement with other parameters of the given equation. For instance,

$N = N_o + N_2 + N_3$ has the exclusion of N_4. $N = N_o + N_3$ has the exclusion of N_1, N_2 and N_4. In other words, $N = N_o + N_3$ represents the individual whose sex life excludes or is not in agreement with the parameters N_1, N_2 and N_4. It is denoted by -.

Chapter Three

Applications and Likely Future Projection

All postulations of human relevance should have areas of applications; fields of knowledge where they can be applied to improving humanity. The Code-13 Principle possesses immense applications to various endeavours (primarily in the social sciences).

By application, this novel work piece can be applied in three major areas of social and scientific analysis namely:

1) Sexology

2) Psychology

3) Sociology

1) Sexology: An appreciation of this come-to-stay development will go a long way in providing a road map for sexologists to carry out comprehensive research on various sexual behaviours of people; taking to account issues of sexual intercourse as it affect their personalities in relation to people (partners) they are engaged with.

2) Psychology: It will serve as reliable helping aid-proffering psychologists with ways of evaluating thought processes of individuals of varying sex lives.

3) Sociology: This will act as an enabling approach for sociologists to label or describe people of different sex lives better and assert dynamic approach patterns to preclude them from the servitude of odds associated with the various sex lives.

Future projection

With modifications and other subsequent attachments, it will go a long way in face-lifting criminology to a pinnacle of all humanity's endeavours. This development will foster (easier) detection of crimes and coupled with forensics, bring about more accurate crime detection strategies which will (in return) curb world crime to its barest minimum. By knowing the sexual personalities of people, crime detection can pin-point likely criminal tendencies they could portray, thereby paving a way for easier crime detection.

Note: At present, it is tentative.

Gender

Housewifery...giving the role of women a professional and an academic touch

Preface

It is an obvious fact that the smallest unit of any society is the family, chief resident of a home (not a house). Of course, the head of the house is the man but the home-maker is the woman. Though a man may acquire magnificent edifices to his enrichment, it takes a 'good' woman to make them homes.

However, the reverse is the case in our contemporary world of civilization where husbands and wives are in pursuit of enhanced convenience at the expense of home building, monetary gains at the expense of physical and mental development of their family members (especially children) and other seen interests. Unequivocally, these discrepancies have truncated stability in most homes thereby constituting inauspicious divorce and estranged issues and eventually broken homes.

At this point, an instance will be necessary to explain the importance of a 'good' home-maker, a woman (precisely a wife). A law is passed into a country's constitution as its recognition. Without the functionality of the executioner, what is the essence or potency of the law? Similarly, a man, the head of the house, can (only) practically pass the instructions to be executed by the woman. Without this, the home will undoubtedly be in shambles. Come to think of it, the executioner is a trained person equipped with the skill of properly executing or acting appropriately on laws passed. In the same vein, a woman or better put, a wife is nurtured with the necessary physical, mental and spiritual empowerment, recognition to deal with issues that face the home. What happens if the woman is not equipped with these empowerment recognition over the years? The answer can be likened to a plant without a functional nucleus. That plant is a phantom!

Realistically, the reason most homes experience estranged and divorce situations is simply because the woman, the nucleus of the home, is not really functional-not properly demonstrating the skills of being called a wife. Wives are trained women, physically mentally and spiritually. In other words, they are specially equipped with the abilities to follow etiquettes; moral, social and spiritual values needed to keep the home alive. By deduction, most men marry physically mature ladies only to discover they are not wife-fit. Hence, the cases of divorce, separation and broken homes emerge. Ponder on this statement: 'if you want to lively and long-lasting home, for your good, marry a wife and not a physically mature lady because she is a field that lures you with her virtues, transforming your manly disposition into an active husband'. Sad to say but the truth; some men who marry physically mature women with time get to know that they are arguably baby-making machines. This is the reason most men seek solace out of the bounds of their matrimony, inviting a host of vices such as divorce, separation and other home-destroying imbalances.

Consequently, children are usually at the receiving end of the issue. The inability of the man and woman to effectively channel their resources together towards the mental, physical and spiritual development of their wards or children is one of the major factors responsible for juvenile delinquencies, moral decadence, armed robbery, increased corruption rate, homosexualism and so on. It hampers parent-children relationships.

Note: In as much as it is the responsibility of the man to ensure the financial and material up-keep of the house, it is duty of the woman to ensure stability (physical, mental and spiritual interests) of the home. If the home-maker is defenseless, that is, not equipped with the stated recognition, the man becomes defenseless and home will eventually be in ruins.

Think about it, if these vices are eminent in our society, are you really safe? Remember, what goes around comes around. You could imagine the negative effects such discrepancies to a country and paint of its image to the international world.

In a busy world as ours, how can we ensure stability in our homes? How do we rightly juxtapose our profession with home affairs? What should be my priority; my home or career? If i forfeit my career, can I still carter for the home? Can my husband carry out the financial obligations of the house alone? Should I forfeit my lucrative profession for housekeeping, is it a decent thing to do in a world as this?

These questions can truly be answered only if the advent of a particular interest is permitted to stay in our midst. 'What is the PARTICULAR INTEREST? A question you may want to ask. Flip this page!

Introduction

'Educate a man, you have only taught one person but educate a woman, you have succeeded in educating a family'. No doubt, this saying has a profound influence on a woman who has given herself to proper spiritual, physical and mental nurturing through the years. However, the thorough appreciation of the stated recognition of training is made possible if women, who wish to experience not only blissful marriages but also stable homes, are prepared to face the challenges that emerge. This feat can possibly be attained by preparing themselves from the days of youth. How?

The advent of the neologism 'Housewifery' is a projected development aimed at giving 'home-makers' an academic and a professional touch. Analogous to mid-wifery, it encompasses the various nurturing recognition needed to keep the home alive and a stable society, at large.

This is the name given to typically interested 'home-makers'; aspiring wives, aspiring mothers, housekeepers and dedicated married women. Simply, the term HOUSEWIFERY is typically professionalizing the role of housewives in nation building and institutionalizing an academic forte for 'home-makers'

The masterpiece has in its recognition two chapters; professional and academic housewifery. Professional housewifery involves a government-assisted and non-governmental influence in form of evaluation of the performances of housewives in terms of socio-cultural behavioural patterns of their children, proper management of home affairs through a stipulated period of comments given by family members, teachers of their children, close neighbours, husbands and other concerned individuals and experts. Also, rewards, bonuses and other advantages that surface after the evaluation exercised will be brought to the spotlight. On the other hand, academic housewifery is class-based and a do-it approach has a 'governing' curriculum on how its dynamics can be disseminated to students. Rewards also await best students in this intended course of study

By extension, Housewifery, if considered, will pose unequivocally huge benefits to world-known celebrities who believe in the potency of 'home-making' as the basis of nation building as it helps them to rightly juxtapose their stardom (fame) with the call-to-duty interest of home-making.

Housewifery is obviously positioned to assisting interested women; aspiring mothers, dedicated housewives, mothers and want-to-be housekeepers to improve, re-conceptualize, if necessary, correct obnoxious notions and practically appreciate the essence of being the home's watchdog.

Chapter 1
Academic Housewifery

Academic Housewifery has three recognition: the mental/psychological, spiritual and physical (moral, economic) empowerment. Before touching its academic perspective, let us examine briefly Housewifery's recognition

a) Physical (moral/economic) empowerment

We have the following:

1) Economy; spending-income expenses; priorities essential for home upkeep, need for ensuring 'surplus' monetary or financial 'left-overs' to finance unplanned future events, making mutual the spending between herandher husband, calculated and up-to-date record keeping of essential expenses in the home.

2) Sexuality: sex education- the importance of fidelity, dress code at different occasions with husband(as it appeals to him), neighbors, extended family members, creating intimate sexual relationship with husband, child-bearing spacing (as agreed by both parties), understanding the sexual demands of husband at different times and spaces, enlightenment on enhancing effective sexual performances for mutual satisfaction, learning a sense of

passionate appreciation after sexual intercourse, bringing the best out of the husband in terms of dressing and performance and how to express passionate love to him, acquiring methods of creatively providing for husbands (during sexual intercourse) a variety of 'skills' to avoid boredom and a likelihood of occurrence of infidelity, exercising sex education to children at adolescence.

3) <u>Mental/psychological empowerment</u>

Establishing inter-personal relationships with people; husband, children, neighbors and other extended family members, perceptions of life issues as it affects the home, coping with mental/emotionally stress/fatigue 'disturbing' household members, temperament control, acquisition of necessary first-aid precaution in case of emergency in the home, acquiring the right cooking techniques of various foods (local and exotic) and eating skills, learning the etiquettes of serving meals to the members of the home (internal and external) and visitors and appreciating the need of consulting counselors, if home-unfriendly issues are difficult to bear, teaching the children the rules of good behaviours from the tender ages, listening to their pleas, questions, complaints, requests and trying as much as possible to see to their wants, if it is within the limits of capability. If there is a misdemeanor in the child or children, acquiring the right scolding technique or subtle punishment tactic will be appreciated. Also, teaching children how to establish inter-personal relationships at tender ages is important; knowing their potentials at these ages and acting on them will be appreciated. Ensuring children's hygiene, medical health through sanitation; do-it yourself clean-up exercises (washing of clothes, plates, 'specialized sweeping' in accordance with the age of children and physical build) time-to-time medical health check-up and ensuring balanced diet will be a great deal. Seeing to the intelligent/academic performances or dispositions by encouraging them to listen to educative programs, news and current affairs, giving them homeworks/assignment, enabling them engage in brain-storming creative games (in the positive sense). In addition, educating them, especially the females on how to employ good cooking techniques at tender ages is allowed.

4) Spiritual empowerment

Teaching the children how to pray

Praying for the going and coming of every family member

Ensuring before any activity, prayers should be made.

Every issue concerning the home should first be put to prayers

In case of sickness, chaos in the home, noticed infidelity and other socio-culturally and unfriendly identities, spiritual exercises such as prayers and fasting are to be implored.

Taking spiritually seriously, every 'unusuality' noticed in every family member

Exercising the habit of continued prayer for the home, state and nation for peace and security

If not spiritually strong, seeking for mentorship from a spiritually mature person will be a great deal.

Teaching the children about the efficacies of prayers, adhering strongly to the tenets of faith associated with the practiced lifestyle (in this case, Christianity) from tender ages.

Spiritually ensuring there is peace and stability in the home and unity amongst family members, neighbors and other concerned individuals

Teaching the children to cope; exercising the heart of forgiveness, if offended by anyone.

The physical, spiritual and mental empowerment will appreciate the recognition of the following experts and more; home economists, sexologists, (Christians) religious scholars, psychologists, marriage counselors, nutritionists or dieticians and other concerned professionals to academically disseminate the efficacies of their wealth of knowledge based on the stated topics (intended courses). A curriculum expert will be needed for the sake of coherent arrangement of the intended courses as they fall under the recognition of spiritual, physical and mental empowerment.

Note: for the economic, the wife has to engage herself in what she knows how to do (vocational endeavours) to supplement the home/family need. Else, it may affect the spending/purchasing power of her husband.

Academically, Housewifery is a three-year programme that has in its recognition, in order of succession, the physical, mental and spiritual empowerment.

First Year Of Study : Physical

i) Economic (physical) empowerment courses

ii) Sexuality (physical) empowerment (courses)

Second Year Of Study: Mental

Mental/Psychological empowerment (courses)

Third Year Of Study

Spiritual Empowerment (courses)

(Project year)

The first, second and third years of study will be project-based. In other words, at the end of the first-year study term, a project, based on the student's interest, will be assigned and in recognition of the exams taken on the various courses, the marks will be graded. For the second year of stud, there would be a do-it-yourself demonstration. Simply, after the duration of the second year programme, students would be assigned to different establishments such as the orphanage homes, hospitals and other non-governmental outfits. Together with the examinations taken, the marks will be graded. Also, outstanding students would be sent o feature in reality-air show programmes with children to test their 'true demonstrative demeanour'. Similarly, taking to cognizance examinations taken, the marks will be graded. At the end of the final year of study, projects, based on students' interests will be assigned and with the already-taken examinations, the marks will be graded.

<u>Prospects/Advantages</u>

1) The government will finance the best student with a huge sum for studentship.

2) Prospective husbands

3) Professional recognition

4) Students of Housewifery, if married, will automatically receive at least 40% discount for 18 years for expenses that have to do with their homes (e.g. utilities).

Chapter 2
Professional Housewifery

This is another recognition given to the come-to-stay interest. It involves the active participation of the following bodies:

1) The nation's government
2) Incorporation of the interest in the ministry of women affairs
3) Voluntary involvement/employment of experts
4) Co-operation of teachers, neighbors and other concerned individuals.

The bodies are interwoven in terms of their functionalities. Simply put, the co-operation of each body is necessary for the professional recognition of the come-to-stay Housewifery. The acceptance of the interest by the institutions of higher learning (especially in the departments of home sciences and management) and the subsequent follow-up as an incorporated term in the ministry of women affairs through the involvement of voluntary or employed contributions or services of concerned experts will professionalize Housewifery. Finally, the co-operation of teachers, neighbors, married men (husbands) and other concerned individuals will also be important. How?

The professionalism of Housewifery brings to the spotlight the contribution or involvement of the mentioned bodies.

We begin with the co-operation of neighbors, married men (husbands), teachers and other concerned individuals. It is fascinating to know that at stipulated times of the year; outstanding housewives will receive huge rewards such as fat sum of money for the financial stability of their homes, discount of utility payments as expenses in their homes, free education for their children till the age of 18, welfare packages for children and assisted financial savings for their children's insurance scheme till the age of maturity (18 years) and other welfare packages. The information given by neighbors, teachers, husbands and other concerned individuals on the competence of the housewives and one-on-one (personal) interviews by experts with husbands and children concerning their wives and mothers respectively would be conducted. This is a house-to-house exercise with information given from the affiliated ministry of women affairs in strategic places of various localities. The recognition, affiliated to the ministry of women affairs, are saddled with the responsibility of getting concise and precise information from teachers, neighbors, husbands and other individuals. In this lies the involvement of experts. The ministry of women affairs will accept the information and carry out necessary processes to dispensing funds and other miscellaneous interests from the desk of the nation's desk.

Note: The concerned individuals refer to family members (extended). It is essential that the affiliated ministry of women affairs recognition get vital house-to-house information concerning housewives and their families

The Quote On Housewifery

" A true wife is a well-nurtured female who has painstakingly tutored herself the essence of self-control (chastity and resultant fidelity) instead of promiscuity, patience instead of haste, decency instead of indecency, endurance instead of surrendering, spirituality instead of carnality, kindness instead of hostility, love instead of hate, sincerity instead of lie, transparency instead of hypocrisy, faithfulness instead of infidelity, posterity instead of attention to prevailing circumstance(s),diligence instead of selfishness, quality education instead of ignorance, humility instead of pride and exerts these virtues (like a magnet field) by luring her husband; transforming him from just being a physically mature male to an active 'husbandly' entity"

Philosophy

Who is Man?

Preface

Without a doubt, man has wondered on the threshold of his personality. He has, with all logical thoughts, asked about who he is through different means; his existence, purpose and approach to issues and treatment of other sub-ordinates. Mankind has in a way unveiled certain answers to what entirely makes it. However, man is really not satisfied or better yet, has not come to the full realization of who he is.

What man has unveiled as answers to what entirely makes him are the figured out trivialities; wealth, happiness, success, companionship and so on* Arguably, these thoughts are believed to assert what man should crave for and demonstrate who he is. On the contrary, these trivialities, though not bad per se, are no commensurate to man's existence.

Now, the question, 'Who is Man?' comes to focus. The right answers proffered will go a long way in illuminating extensively man's viewpoints concerning his purpose of existence and approach to handling issues and treating other subordinates.

Therefore, 'Who is Man?' annunciates to all mankind the desired (rights) answers with proofs through easy-to-relate-with examples. It is the greatest anticipation and hope that this material will immensely influence the perception of those whose thoughts about mankind are myopic and parochial and rightly position man on the threshold of attaining the light of who he is.

*Is contained in the literary piece, titled 'What Should We Crave for in Life'? by the same author.

Introduction

'Who is Man?' is a work-piece that elucidates the entirety of mankind in terms of who he is, what he has and where he resides. Using simple instances, it intends reaching the bull's eye.

It gives a crux of three major interests concerning man. Analogous to a house owned by Mr. X, say, containing expected facilities such as electronic gadgets, tiles, bedrooms, living room(s), guest room(s), kitchen(s) and so on and Mr. X lives in that house, the identity explains in vivid terms the seemingly hard-nut to crack question; 'Who is Man'?

At this point, there are basic paraphrased assertions that need to be noted. On these bases, the 'Who is Man?' conceptualization will emerge:

The house owner is Mr. X. He lives in a building owned by him. His house contains electronic gadgets, tiles, bedrooms, living -room(s), guest room(s), kitchen(s) and so on. Perhaps, being a visitor who does not know the way to Mr. X's residence, though very important his house address, your interest essentially lies in seeing him.

In the same vein, being 'new' in this field of acquisition, our goal is primarily focused on answering the question, 'Who is man'? The diagram below gives a three-dimensional analysis of the term 'man'.

Spirit (+)

Fig. 1

                                Body (+)

Soul (+)   Not Drawn to Scale

Notice that the soul and body axis are relatively at the horizontal planes while the spirit axis is at the vertical plane. Why? Here the lines across the soul, body and spirit axis represent the level of quality of information, ascertaining the receptiveness of the soul, the build-up of the spirit and bodily reactions in terms of demonstrated actions. Obviously, the three axes are interwoven such that they depend on each other for a 'function' at their respective dimensions. How?

Consider a typical modern-day personal computer. The processor, otherwise known as the brain of the computer, gets information or data from the input device (keyboard, say) and delivers the information as output (through the Visual Display Unit, VDU). Similarly, the soul is comparatively the processor that acts on information received and delivers, determining the orientation of the spirit and body actions. Fig. 2 is a schematic sketch explaining the position of the soul as the yielding-information processor to the spirit and body.

D

Fig.2

Not Drawn To Scale

A　　　　　　B　　　　　　C

　　　　　　　　　　　　　　　　E

KEY

A- Information that reaches the soul

B- The soul processing the information

C- The soul delivering the information to…

D- The spirit (determining its orientation) and

E- The body (affected by the orientation of the spirit).

The soul, spirit and body dimensions tend toward the positives. Therefore, it is anticipated good and quality information which the soul receives, processes and delivers to the spirit and body (which can be translated as the eventual upright service to humanity). However, consider Fig.3 where the three dimensional axis tend towards the negatives.

　　　　　　　　　　　　　　Soul (-)

Fig. 3

Body (-)　　　　　　　Not drawn to scale

　　Spirit (-)

By implication, the soul receives negative information, process and delivers them to the spirit that then determines the body's response or reaction (action). It follows that a debasing service to humanity and declining spiritual growth become the aftermath. In comparison with Fig. 2, the lines in Fig. 3 have the same meanings.

Remember, the soul houses the mind; the thought and action factory. This is a worthy-of-note statement.

Have you heard of the following assertions:

1) Man is a spirit
2) He lives in a body
3) He has a soul?

'Who is man' is an interest that builds its uniqueness on the stated three premises with insight-based statements and down-to-earth instances. The concise-yet-very salient chapters are arranged in the following order:

Chapter 1: Man is a spirit

Chapter 2: He lives in a body

Chapter 3: He has a soul

It is expected the outright conviction of the reader of this classic about the assertions as answers to the question 'Who is man'? This, the author believes, should explain his existence, purpose and treatment (handling) of other subordinates.

Chapter One

Man Is A Spirit

When you desire to know the house address of your friend, you are not necessarily knowing his address but identifying with him or her as occupant of the building. Also, if you are a regular consumer of the soft drink, Coca-Cola, though you have the bottle, your concern is to drink the content (liquid).

In the same vein, in identifying who man is, we must concern ourselves with his 'name'. By the way, have you come across the term 'inner man'? Many pundits of various meta-physical convictions are familiar with this phrase. It is a term used to describe the reality of man. In other words, 'inner man' refers to the originality of man. How? What about those whose convictions are not in agreement with this description?

Undoubtedly, we are familiar with the Homo Abilies nature of man; man's ability to stand upright and better reason distinctly from other created (living) entities. In fact, the upright man (you and I, as we were made to believe) is the Homo Abilies because this is who he is. Similarly, the 'upright' man is a spirit. Here, 'upright' is an adjective used to refer to God's creation- the God-created man.

Even if you do not believe in God, at some point, you, perhaps, through deep thinking, would have (tentatively) seen to a fact that the 'orchestrator' of the universe is obviously no mere man. Rather, 'He' possesses an extra-terrestrial disposition. In succinct terms, 'He' is a spirit. If the 'orchestrator' of the universe created an order of dynamics in the rightly structuralized universe, then the creation of man was also possible. Not only that, the 'orchestrator', being extra-terrestrial in nature, originally made man in such an orientation. Don't you think so? Come to think of it, man acts as an extra-terrestrial being to other subordinates; his subjects and other entities he has dominion over (e.g. plants, animals). This is a reflection of character of the extra-terrestrial being.

The wisest book in the world, the Holy bible, in its account, tells us that God created the heavens and the earth (Genesis 1:1) and more importantly, breathe life into man and man became a living being (Genesis 2:7). The 'life' breathe into man was the life of the spirit. Without it, there was really no need for man's true existence.

Are you aware of the fact that the earth is controlled by spiritual forces and governed by spiritual laws? If you believe so, then what become of your real you? The oblivion of this truth has limited man to the extent he cannot see anything possessing spiritual worth- (over-) prioritizing what he sees. Hence, the craving for trivialities.

A spirit being dwells in eternity. In other words, this real man's name is extra-terrestrial that is completely cut off from the limiting earthly time. He resides at the fourth dimension, a limitation of the earth's physically known 3-dimensional plane. In clear terms, the perfected seven spiritual planes are the dwellings of man's true name. The fourth dimension is the threshold of the other dimensions of the spirit, whether in the positive or negative. Man's spirituality is determined by the operation it best functions. For instance, if the spirit dwells in either the faith or doubt planes, then the level of spirituality has its operational functionality at the faith or doubt dimension.

Moreover, many creative inventions by men that exceed physical scientific explanations are made possible, courtesy of inspiration; a spiritual undertone. This is the movement of spirit that gives man the impetus to propel in such a way as to bring about an unusual masterpiece of creation or change to his world. Without a doubt, science cannot, in concrete terms, explain such efficacies. This is because the knowledge gained and creativity driven through inspiration is connected with spiritual sources which unequivocally transcend the comprehension of science about them.

It is in the spirit man realizes the importance of certain physically unseen forces that constitute a life-long impact on earth; faith, joy, wisdom, wealth, truth, prosperity and so on (Also, the exact opposite of the terms used included) which goes beyond the physically seen things of the world. No wonder the physical man is left between the devil and deep blue sea when the recognition of this matter is brought before him. A wealthy man, irrespective of how he acquired wealth, is a product of 'act-the-faith' exercise which had been aforementioned and executed in the spiritual realm, translating to what he's been addressed as; 'a wealthy man'.

The 'upright' man is the real man who is the spirit. The diagrams demonstrate the assertion.

$$(+)$$

Fig. 4   Spirit Man

Where Spirit Man (+) = Real Man (+) = 'Upright' Man (+)

Not Drawn To Scale

The horizontal lines across the vertical plane represent the dimensions of the spirit (in the positives)

Spirit Man (-)

Fig 5

The lines across represent

The dimensions of

The spirit (in the negatives)

Where Spirit Man (-) = Real Man (-) = 'Upright man' (-)

Here, the negatives and positives respectively represent the 'good' (as in faith, wealth, wisdom, knowledge and so on) and 'bad' (as in their exact opposite) spiritual realms.

The quest and eventual acquisition of all-there-are-to-life trivialities have unequivocally made men and women realize disdain in the form of unfulfilment. Simply, they feel an empty space or vacuum in their lives, despite living in their abundance (money, companionship, certifications and so on. Obviously, what they fail to see is the inability to 'equip' the emptiness they feel in their lives. The not-equipped vacuum in the 'inner man' or spirit, which, if not equipped with information or truths to fill the empty space, will result in obnoxious aftermaths in their lives. Ask yourself this question; 'who is a full-grown man without a name'?

The spirit cannot relate with the physical. The physical, being a 'solidified' 3-dimensional plane, agrees on a relationship with a being that is also physical. By nature, the liquid content of the Coca-Cola bottle can move freely. But it has to be encased in a bottle for proper consumption; value for money. Also, the house owner needs his house to lay his head, at least. Similarly, man, originally a spirit being, needs a 'casing' to relate with the physical. This takes us to the next chapter.

Chapter Two
He Lives In A Body

As recognized, the liquid content of a Coca-Cola bottle has to be encased in a solid for proper consumption. A house owner needs his house to lay his head. In the same vein, the body is the casing that the spirit is domicile and 'encased' for a proper relationship with the physical world.

The body can relate easily with the physical world, earth, thanks to the functional presence of the human sense organs. As a matter of fact, the human body is a perfect match to the natural world!

As aforementioned, the body is a 'casing' which practically demonstrates thoughts and actions. By primarily writing, gesticulating or involving itself in certain 'do-it' activities, the body attains the bull's eye. Of course, thanks to the senses it has.

To relate perfectly with the physical world and successfully create and impact or occupy and balance the earth's eco-system, it must be living. Also, for the proper functioning of the human sense organs responsible for the physical activities in the world, the nucleus, which is the engine room of the body, has to be present. The nucleus, analogous to the liquid content, which is the 'life' of the Coca-Cola bottle, is the human blood.

Therefore, it will be impossible for man to relate with the physical world without the presence of blood. Afterall, the life of the physical man is in the blood. This implies that for the continued existence of mankind to demonstrate its unique thoughts and actions, the ever-present human blood is undoubtedly essential.

The demonstrated thoughts and actions could tend towards the negatives or positives, depending on the quality of information received.

Fig. 6

Body (-)

Body (-)

The arrow signs represent the realistic good and atrocious deeds of humanity over the millennia, centuries or decades, as the case may be.

Consider a brand-new car with no driver. Obviously, as the Newtonian law of motion states, it will exhibit inertia-the reluctance to move when it is static. In a way, the instance is akin to the human body with no 'driver'. Then, who is the 'driver'? No doubt, without the consent of the 'driver', the human body cannot physically reach the destination of demonstrating its unique thoughts and actions. Interestingly, the driver and his brand-new car (the 'driver' and human body, in a respectively compared analogy) all operate on the horizontal (physical) plane.

The next chapter discusses the essentiality of the 'driver' as it affects the thought and action processes demonstrated by the human body.

Chapter Three

He Has a Soul

The ability of the human body to relate with the physical world via demonstrated thoughts and actions is made possible by the soul possessed by man. The soul, in agreement with the body, makes the relationship existing between the 3-dimensional world and humanity possible.

Considering the building owned by Mr. X, Mr. X would normally lay his head inside it because the building's interior has living room(s), bedroom(s) and other accommodation-friendly facilities. The Coca-Cola drink contains special constituents such as carbonated water, carbon dioxide and other preservatives that bring about its unique taste. In a similar fashion, man has a soul responsible for his ability to think and act physically using his body (in agreement).

In a sense, the soul 'houses' the mind. With respect to the previously given example, the house owned by Mr. X is the soul and its interior is the mind. No matter the look-alike exterior look of the house owned by Mr. X and those of others, there are differences, one way or the other. Also, the interiors are uniquely different.

Therefore, the soul is what makes the physically unique man. In other words, the soul is the:

S-Source

O-Of

U-Unparalled

L-Lure

This is responsible for the 'drawing' of people of different social, economic and political interests toward identifying with and ardently following cut-across-all-barriers ideologies, postulated by an individual or a group of people. However, the soul's engine room is the mind. The need to look into the soul's nucleus becomes undoubtedly essential.

The mind, an essential component of the human soul, is akin to the computer processor, responsible for the processing of information from the input (keyboard, say) and delivers it as output through the output device (Visual Display Unit, VDU). The mind receives information, processes it, ascends it to the spirit and create an enabling environment for the body to practically think and act on it, whether in the positives or negatives.

The diagram below shows a driver-in-a-vehicle stance, explaining the closeness of the mind and body.

Fig. 6

A Driver

Vehicle

E

Here, the driver A is the mind and vehicle is the body. Obviously, without the driver, the vehicle will remain static and without the vehicle, the driver cannot showcase his driving skill. Precisely, without the mind, the body cannot relate with the physical and without the body, the mind cannot pilot demonstrated thoughts and actions. In all, they are sine qua non to each other. Notice: the arrow sign (E) indicates the driver and vehicle are on a horizontal plane. Hence, the reason for the sine qua non relationship.

The mind exhibits its 'driving skill' by:

M-Meditating

I-Intensively,

N-Never

D-Declining. The ability of the mind to depict its most outstanding quality or 'driving skill' is a reflection of its processing power on information received (knowledge) and delivering it to the 'appropriate' quarters for their respective dimensional functions, despite oppositions or inevitable odds (in the positives or negatives).

Figures 7 and 8 show the mind (soul) and body axes as found along the horizontal plane.

Fig. 7 Body (+)

Soul (mind)

(+)

Body (-)

Fig. 8

Soul (Mind)

All symbols have their usual meanings.

Interestingly, God made man in such a creative fashion such that MAN;

M-Meta-physically

A-Ascends

N-Naturally.

In other words, man's 'upright' positioning is spiritual; meaning that man is a spirit. However, in order to relate with the 3-dimensional world of his existence, the agreement between the body and soul (mind) must be established. The 3-dimensional operating human body must be stretched beyond its naturally recognized limits through the active Meditating Intensively, Never Declining Quality of the mind, thereby ascending processed information to the spirit which eventually ascertains the body's level of ascertained thoughts and actions.

Always Remember These: The spiritual controls the physical. The man-spirit control is made possible courtesy of the information processed by the mind and acted on by the body.

All constructive criticisms towards the improving the quality of this write-up are welcome. Afterall, the essence of involving readers is to enable them know more than the writers who masterminded the works in their possession.

Education

The Apparently Creeping Disappearance of Reading Culture In Modern Times

Preface

Over the years, it has been thought that the black man is a described race whose attitude towards book reading has experienced a decline from the turmoil of the slavery age to our era. As a matter of fact, it said that one of the ways of denying a typical black man of quality information is to write it in a book. However, as the years progress, it is factual that other races have shown not-encouraging interests towards reading books , perhaps, owing to changing times of world's demands. The question, arising from this development:'what factors are responsible'? comes to focus.

No doubt, book-reading culture is the bedrock of all man's witty inventions, etiquettes, fundamentals of socio-political norms, solutions to imminent socio-political and economic challenges and so on. Yet, it has, it is and if not properly looked into, will be extinct in a not-too-distant future.

It has come to the notice that people have prioritize other interests ahead of the fundamentally important book-reading but failed to realize it constitutes the essence of their priorities, Consequently, the preference given to these interests (materialism, for instance) will lead to information deficiency amongst individuals, especially the leaders of tomorrow's world, the today's growing youths.

As we approach the information and knowledge age proper, the essentiality of book-reading undoubtedly positions itself as the pivot to surmount challenges, associated with these ages. People's complacent attitude towards the culture of book reading will mentally, spiritually, socially and physically stagnate their ability to commensurate the demands of these ages.

At this juncture, a question needs to be asked: 'do you really read quality books; books that are of positive influence in your life?' If yes, congratulations! If not, then we have to identify the factors responsible for your not reading books.

Mr. Ben

Introduction

The Apparently Creeping Disappearance of Reading Culture In Modern Times sheds light on reasons people are longer reading books as they used to. It is a three-chapter write-up that unveils three major reasons the reading culture has experienced a near-extinction over the years. Therefore, it asserts the need for its resuscitation or thorough existence but maintains a stance that the attitude of book reading is choice-based.

The three-chapter material which gives three major reasons for the decline in book reading is arranged in the following formats:

Chapter One-Reason One-Parental Incompetence

Chapter Two-Reason Two-Quest for wealth, Riches, money or material gains

Chapter Three-Reason Three-Pressure on youths to prioritize academic pursuits over book reading.

In summary, Reasons One, Two and Three are to be detailed with insight-based fats and instances (examples and stories)

In a nutshell, the work seeks the need for complete attention towards book reading; the bedrock of all man's inventions, answers to questions, way of life and more importantly, basis of existence.

Chapter One

Reason One

<u>Parental Incompetence</u>

The saying: 'charity begins at home' is unequivocally correct. Precisely, the saying can simply be put this way: 'book-reading culture starts from the home-front'. Therefore, the chief residents of the home, that is, parents, play pivotal roles in properly nurturing their children or wards in the light of book reading. In other words, inculcating the attitude of book reading in children is a demanding task parents meet.

However, it has been observed that modern-day parents have somewhat forgotten the importance of inculcating the book reading culture in the growing years of their children. Rather, they either subjugate them to doing other things like carrying out house chores; typical of parents in third-world countries or by liberal standards, allow their children go beyond the limits of watching T.Vs during the nights, surfing the internet without stern supervision or attending parties regularly. These dispositions by parents towards their children do not favour the thriving of the essentially important and should-be-appreciated book reading culture.

The inability of parents to properly nurture their children in the recognition of the culture of book reading is vividly a factor responsible for intellectual deficiency in children's ability to comprehend what they are taught in and off the classroom. A situation where a parent cannot inculcate the habit of book reading in the growing years of his or her children or wards will automatically anticipate intellectually and information-deficient adults who will pose liabilities to the societies they find themselves.

As a parent, imagine a situation where your children are fond of watching T.V programs, depicting obscene and non-educative messages instead of paying rapt attention to their books. Without strict supervision, what do you expect of your children when they become adults?

The Bible warns parents to train their children the way they ought to go. In other words, it admonishes parents to diligently impose values essential to their proper physical, mental, social and spiritual development. These values can verily be found in books because the bible is a divinely written and inspiration-based book Thus, equipping children with the right social, physical and spiritual values entails the involvement of parents to diligently inculcate inevitable values to their children by habituating them to edifying books e.g. the Holy bible, Quran and so on. Sincerely, how many parents have come to the cognizance of this truth?

A factor that encourages parental incompetence, paving the way for the decline of book reading in children is the imbalance of the home. A home where the parents, whose visions are diverted, will experience division which brings about complacency in the attitude of their children towards reading. Also, a home where there is a single parent (single mother or father) as the chief resident will without a doubt not be able to properly enforce the culture of book reading on its children, perhaps, owing to pressing socio-economic demands. No wonder children whose remarkable performances are accountable to the mutual and painstaking efforts of their parents to discipline them in the light of reading quality books, instrumental for their academic excellence. On the other hand, the reverse becomes the case to children with low academic performances.

Therefore, the home, a nucleus or foundational block of any society, should recognize the vital role of its chief residents, the parents (precisely, the man and wife or better yet, mother and father) in the proper nurturing of their children physically, socially and spiritually towards raising responsible and productive individual for the society. This feat can be achieved by primarily identifying with the lifestyle or culture of book reading.

Interestingly, children learn fast from things they easily gain access to knowing this fact; it is disheartening why many parents directly or indirectly allow their wards to have access to certain materials or technologies whose messages portray decadence without strictly 'sieving' what they access.

Instead of watching non-educative and negatively entertainment programs on air, why can't parents take their time to monitor and shape the thinking towards positively entertaining and edifying programs? Remember, the joy of parents is to see their children excel in their endeavours. The possibility is a reality only if they can place them during their growing years the diet of book reading.

To this moment, you, as an adult, are a product of your past experiences. More importantly, you are a reflection of values acquired through the growing years of human development (infancy, childhood, adolescence, and adulthood), primarily through the books you read and company you keep. The quality of thoughts and actions you possess is therefore a result of the culmination of past experiences, predominately a function of childhood experiences spelt out in the kind of books you read in relation to the interaction with your peers and people around you.

I remembered a friend of mine in primary school whose parents were always busy that they rarely give him attention. Rather, they diligently sought for monetary and material possession. He was left alone at the mercy of a spoilt housemaid who pampered him with excess obscene materials; magazines, nude pictures of herself and X-rated videos. At a tender age of six, he was exposed to different immoral acts.

In school, it was precisely a fateful Friday morning when our class teacher asked each pupil the question: 'what is the capital of Norway'? Luckily for me, i have at the time mastered most countries' capitals in Europe. When it got to my turn, i replied 'Oslo!' Funny enough, he replied, 'eroticity!', when asked the same question.

At the end of the class, after being asked a series of questions by our head teacher who was told about the development, it was discovered he watched porn movies ardently and what he writes in his books and communicate to his peers are words associated with pornography, a reflection of the information acquired watching the movies. Also, our head teacher discovered his complacent attitude towards reading quality books given to him.

Later, our head teacher summoned his parents to explain reasons behind the not-good character of their child. After all said and done, he had to go through intense rehabilitation and subsequent efforts such as habituating him in the light of book reading and subsequent efforts were geared by his parents and our teachers to ensure behavioral change.

Today, he is grateful for the effort made by his parents. As I write this work piece, he is a responsible married man, humanitarian and successful business man.

Chapter Two

Reason Two

<u>Thirst or craze for material, financial, riches or wealth acquisition</u>

I was on my way to visiting a friend when i overheard a fully grown adult say to himself; 'money is all there is to life. In fact, the bible asserts that money answers all things and is a defence. Therefore, I must go and make money at all cost, by crook or by hook'. Indeed, these assertions point to another reason the craze or thirst for material, financial or wealth acquisition has been at its height over the years, perturbing the essentially important book reading.

A good of friend of mine, name withheld, decided to 'drop out' of high school to take the profession of a police recruit. For almost a decade he had been in the force, he still encounters difficulties in actually writing a complete sentence! Then, he believed he could scale through the ranks of the force through cut-corner means and in the process, part away with fortunes. Although he was successful at getting what was aimed at, the deficit of illiteracy still lingers. In future, if he fails to inculcate the habit of book reading, he stands a chance of being out-smarted by clever and educated individuals.

Generally, the thirst for materialism has unequivocally being registered in the psyche of people, irrespective of age, race or background. In other words, the craze for money, riches or wealth has made many individuals belief in the essentiality of these trivialities over their emanation. Simply, many peoples of the world have shown parochial and myopic viewpoints into believing that money is all there is to living a fulfilled life.

To this effect, men and women go extra miles at the expense of their lives and the lives of others to ensure they attain financial opulence. Without a doubt, we hear of cases of respected men and women of rectitude dragging their originally written-in-gold names to the mud, all in the name of wealth or riches by fraudulent means.

Of course, what they fail to identify is the source behind the potency or power of monetary or wealth acquisition. Simply put, many money-hungry people cannot in concrete terms pinpoint the source of money or how money came to existence. They do not know what should rather be prioritized money or its source.

If you were to use the question 'what is money?' to X-ray many people (within your sphere contact, at least), you will be surprised at the responses you would get. Some would respond, saying something like: 'money is life', 'money is the world in my control', 'money is the substance used for the purchase 0f my need', 'money is a respect-earner, power-giver and influence-seeker' and so on. Arguably, they are right in their opinion and entitled to their viewpoints. However, do these expressions really assert the concept or meaning of money?

Interestingly, the concept behind the genuinty of the term 'money' is embedded in books! Only those who are boo-reading-conscious can unravel the concept and origin of the world's most acceptable medium of exchange. How?

At this juncture, the question that should be asked is: 'what is the purpose of money'? The right response asked will certainly go a long way in questioning the viewpoint of men and women who have stagnated their minds to believing the mirage 'money is everything'.

In history, there were various forms of exchange for goods and services, ranging form the medieval period to the late 1800s, in different locations of the world. In some parts, cowries were used and precious substances such as gold, silver, platinum were used in other parts of the world. In one sentence, the trade-by-barter approach to business was generally accepted exchange meant at those times.

However, realizing the disadvantages, inconveniencies and other imbalances, pundits, scholars erudite and other history's respected intellectuals sat together over the years to brainstorm and unanimously agree on a much-less inconveniencing, nearly no-disadvantageous medium of exchange which would become a universally phenomenon.

It was not until 1919 that the use of paper money was birth into the world with the intent of serving as the means of exchange for goods and services, its most outstanding quality. In fact, many economists agree with this assertion! By deduction, goods and services are a product of witty inventions and ideas of people that are being exchanged via the use of the tool called money.

Where can one get access to these facts? Books! Ideas, commercially translated as goods and services in the form of witty inventions and strategic definitions, have made the existence of man worth living are embedded in books. The advantage of book reading in terms of thorough study is the enablement to generate world-changing ideas that will engender not only desired changes but also huge fortunes and opportunities. Really, if you claim you have an idea about something, you can only be sure of its authenticity by consulting a guiding and corresponding written material (book).

A good way of elucidating the economist's most outstanding quality of money can be creatively analyzed as MONEY, that is;

M-Means (Medium)

O-Of

N-(inter)National

E-Exchange (for)

Y-Yields

Money, in the light of its most outstanding quality, can be defined as the means or medium of local and/or foreign exchange for yields (goods, services a statement of profitably translated ideas).

In other words, money is a tool or servant (in a way) to ideas. And world-changing ideas are an appreciation of book reading via study. In itself, money can best be rightly used by knowing its emanation (which has its chronology written in books). Always remember this: ideas rule the world.

Chapter Three

Reason Three

<u>Pressure on youths to prioritize academic pursuits over book reading</u>

Not bad the pursuit of academic accomplishment, the pressure on youths especially at tertiary levels to place priorities over the essentially important book reading leaves much to be desired. Tertiary institutions such as the universities, monotechnics, and polytechnics and so on have made cumbersome and stereotyped academic workloads on students that they rarely have time for themselves, let alone reading edifying books. However, is this way to attain academic goals?

During our growing years, we were made to believe hook, line and sinker that a thorough academic education; primary, secondary and tertiary education will enable us attain job security, huge salaries, create a high standard of living, reduce social and economic vices, help us find solutions to impending challenges, make us rich in future and enable us properly take good care of our families and contribute our quota towards the development of our countries. Good reasons behind having a thorough education. But there is a missing factor... 'What's that?' A good question!

As observed, the world is changing. Therefore, the need for social, cultural and political faces of the world are experiencing change; economic turmoil is rocking many nations, there is a drastic fall in educational standards in many countries (particularly third-world countries), unemployment of tertiary graduates and incessant retrenchment of workers by private outfits and public parastatals and prestigious multi-national companies, increasing moral decadence and delinquencies amongst youths (especially the literates), looming poverty existing in developing nations whose citizens are academically literates, unforetold and unchecked slash in workers' salary scale, high divorce rates and spousal abuse, divided or broken homes and little or no contribution to societal development. Yet, youths are unnecessary pressured over academic accomplishments over book reading.

Let us zero in our case study on tertiary institutions in Africa, precisely Nigeria. It has been observed that students who instead of studying their books, read and learn on a superficial basis; the psyche of cramming with the intention of writing verbatim what their lecturers have taught them during the course of the semester, only to forget after the examination period is over. The repeated superficial learning during the duration of the studied course (sometimes, four, five, six academic years excluding strike and internal problems) have produced an army of information-stagnant graduates who lag behind the fast-rising gradient of world development . Obviously, they cannot compete with their foreign counterparts. Rather, instead of being nurtured as job creators, they become eventual job seekers, unnecessarily 'polluting' the labour market; a crowd of job seekers vying for limited job spaces available. In all, the few lucky or successfully employed ones are left at the mercy of their employers who seem to hold the key to their fortunes in future. What about the majority? Unemployed, of course! Breathing decadence, insecurity and total liability to the society, the jobless but academically certified youth among others are arguably headed toward these directions.

On second thought, would you really blame students who have imbibed the superficial learning habit when there is little or no time to read life-building books, 'loaded' with apparently insurmountable and take-your-time assignments, projects and other commitments that seem not to have changed? Given a number of courses that carry huge units and other borrowed courses which are made compulsory but really unnecessary pertaining to the course of study, if you were in this situation, how do you want to read life-changing books?

The earlier we realize that academic education ends in the fore-walls of the classroom and pose little or no practical consequences to typical life issues, the better. Nowadays, academic education can only create a meaningful impact to the lives of learning youths if those in charge of the system can lift a ban of stereotypic and cliché-based learning by seeking for interests focused on improving the existence of humanity by continually modifying or making better already-used-to endeavours. The straight-to-life applications of modified or improved academic teachings can only be found in life-edifying books, an appreciation of (quality) book reading, tantamount to qualitative education. 'Qualitative education?' How do you mean?

Qualitative education is basically a do-it-yourself mindset approach. The ability of an individual to develop his or her potentials through the years of academic study will ascertain how accomplished such an individual would be. Loosely speaking, qualitative education is a life-long education which involves a continued development of unearthed potentials for the purpose of rightly serving God and Humanity.

Therefore, an individual developing certain potentialities is without a doubt investing in his or her personality. This is primarily as a result of the quality of books read, a showcase of qualitative education in association with the company kept.

I do not know what you see to this view but I believe in the efficacy of this assertion: the school should be seen as a platform or threshold where students can decide what is best for them. Here, 'the school' refers to the institution of higher learning. 'How can i decide what's best for me when my academic workload is much'? A question you may ask.

The following give an overview of the milestone achievements of individuals who have exercised the essence of qualitative education. Remember, success comes with a prize (an eventuality of quality education) and you can only discover this by reading books.

Bill Gates, CEO, Microsoft Inc. had to leave the prestigious Harvard University to pursue his life-long dream. Now, he is one of the recognized richest entrepreneurs in the world. The products of his company; various Microsoft packages are presently cannot-do-without educational tools used in classrooms.

Thomas Edison only had three months of formal education but he is the greatest inventive person ever. To his credit, he has precisely 1, 093 patents. Amongst his inventions is the popular electric bulb that took over nine hundred failed attempts. The advancement of the electric bulb has made classroom lectures arguably worth enjoying

Ted Turner, CEO of one of the world's most recognized Cable National Network, CNN, was a school drop-out but through personal development demonstrated as elf-investment, he was able to carve a niche for himself in the world of broadcasting.

The Wright Brothers had no formal education. Interestingly, personal development in terms of experiences gathered enabled them successfully invent the first locomotive, air-friendly object, the Airplane, in 1903

Although a right attitude towards academics is very important, it is unequivocally vital and obvious the importance of habitual book reading to properly cope with life issues should be implemented in schools to bring about productive and world-changing individuals.

As the great William Shakespeare observed, 'if you are not informed, you are deformed', It follows that the difference between you, as of present and in future will primarily be determined by the quality of books you read and the company you keep. Although it is a matter of choice, embracing the culture of book reading will be great deal.

Business

Business Success (The 7 'unavoidables' to succeeding in Business)

Preface

- Ever wondered why the United States of America and other first-world nations are of the world's business strong-holds? Do you want to know why few people excel in their business endeavours, despite opposing odds while others, giving the best of auspicious conditions, achieve a tip of the anticipated iceberg or even fail gallantly? Do you really want to the core facts associated with successful business giants? If you really want to know in-depth the secretly-held-onto facts associated with business success, then it is a step in the right direction to read between the lines of this article.

- Preparing a sumptuous meal involves a careful selection of the right ingredients with an expertise-driven approach. Similarly, being successful in business or experiencing mega business success involves a careful consideration and demonstration of the right inevitable, constituting the facts necessary for business growth. Interestingly, the consideration and demonstration of the right 'unavoidables' are the only major difference that widens the gap between successful business giants and not – growing business "dwarfs". What are the right 'unavoidables'?

- Have you considered the uniqueness of the number "7"? Believe it or not, the number "7" is apparently a mystery to some people in terms of its particular uniqueness but really a symbol of perfection. In a larger picture, the right inevitables are the perfected "7" recognition, that is, *The 7 'unavoidables' to succeeding in Business.* Simply, the difference between successful and non-successful ones is the ability to carefully consider and demonstrate *The 7 'unavoidables' to succeeding in Business.* Without a doubt, the U.S and other developed nations has over the years recognized the perfected "seven" recipes necessary for continued thriving and advancement of every business endeavours, a simple statement of business success.

Introduction

The title, *Business Success (The 7 'unavoidables' to succeeding in Business)* gives facts that make business success impossible without proper consideration and demonstration of the perfected seven 'unavoidables'. In simple terms, it is a mini-sized business guide to all individuals, irrespective of endeavours, age, race, status or background engaged in the world of business.

- It is a seven-chapter work-piece that shields high on each of the "cannot-do-withouts", necessary for business success. In other words, a chapter represents an irrefutable fact. It is a fascinating succession of each of the chapters; a one-step at a time definition of the irrefutable facts of business success. In clear terms, every chapter is a follow-up of the preceding one. For instance, chapter two is a "next" to chapter one.

Chapter one

Defining the Orientation Of Business.

- If you a listener of any T.V, radio and other media-assisted commercials of Nokia Phones, what do you hear? "Connecting people". If you are a regular consumer of sprite, what you would hear is "Obey your thirst" A typical peak milk consumer knows the slogan of peak milk: "it's in you". A social "There is a drop of greatness in every man". These enterprises portray one thing: they are able to define the orientation of their interest through their advert slogan. How do an individual define the orientation of his business enterprise? A question you may ask.

- The bible recognizes the essence of defining purposes associated with business activities; "Write your vision; make it plain so that people may run through it". Therefore, defining the dynamics of business involves the basic recognition of vision and mission statements. In other worlds, making plain by writing explicating the vision and mission statements defines the business kind in terms of target audience reach production, distribution, publicity, profitability, comsumability of product, and other intentions. By identifying with the vision and mission statements, an individual is said to witness a face-lift as in them lie aims, objectives, goals, creed, policies, rules and regulations which are the most primary fact associated with business success.

- To demonstrate the power of vision and mission statements, let us consider this instance. This instance will demystify some of the business associated facts. A certain individual in the middle of a very dark night was about setting out to his abode from a very distant location without a car and no money for transport. However, he had an electrically powered touch light which he used all through the journey to his residence. Note certain assertions:

a) "…in the middle of a very dark night…"

b) "…setting out to his abode from a very distant location without a car and no money for transport."

c) "…electrically powered touch light…"

d) "…without a car and no money…"

In the light of business focus, "in the middle of a very dark night" can be interpreted as the yet – to – be – gathered bits and pieces of defining the orientation of business. "setting out to his abode from a very distant location without a car and no money for transport" means writing plain the vision and mission statement leading to success attainment without necessarily being spoon-feed by financially opulent individuals for succor and/or "fish-fed" by experienced business consultants to write on the concerned individual's behalf the vision and mission statements of the his or her business. "electrically powered touch light" simply means the guiding mission and vision statements.

On the other hand, imagine a situation where an individual decides not to switch off his or her electrically powered torchlight and walk home in the middle of that very dark night to his abode from the distant location. Do you think such an individual will make it to his abode? What do you may likely happen on his way home? Don't you think he is treading on the part of absolute obscurity a pointer of ambiguity, a haphazard and not- the- way-home route?

In reality, this is what primarily widens thegap between mega successful businesses giants and the (seemingly) not-growing business "dwarfs".Successful business people take as paramount (for starters) the essence of appreciating the statements of their mission and vision, the guide lights to the success experienced in their business. They have been able to demonstrate a fact: vision statement gives a practical guide on the right approach to the mission statement. In other words, they act on the principle that states: acting on the stated vision through mission, unveiled by the mission statement is a key used in driving the vehicle of any business to the destination of anticipated success. On the other side of the coin, the (seemingly) not-growing business "dwarfs" experience unrelenting setbacks in their business because of not-properly-structured and the followed mission and vision statements. To an extent, this is the reason people fail in businesses: treading the part of ambiguity (Obscurity) instead of constructing their intended business specifics (mission and vision statements).

If you are passionate about something and you intend making is a source of livelihood, then, you are advised to make it a business success by first creating its vision and mission, in the form of statements-a product of your strategy. Also, if you are literate enough, that is, having the ability not only to read and write, but learn and be teachable, then, you can write out your vision (what you want to do with you are passionate about actualizing your vision).

What's next after the mission and vision statements must have been properly structured (written down)? A question you may want to ask. Of course, acquiring knowledge or knowing the intricacies surrounding the uniqueness of what you are about engaging in because paramount. Simply, the acquisition of knowledge is the next step, a follow-up of your constructed vision and mission statements, a subsequent and one of the not-do-without to defining the orientation of your meant-to-be successful business.

Chapter Two
Defining The Orientation Of Business.

- If you a listener of any T.V, radio and other media-assisted commercials of Nokia Phones, what do you hear? "Connecting people". If you are a regular consumer of sprite, what you would hear is "Obey your thirst" A typical peak milk consumer knows the slogan of peak milk: "it's in you". A social "There is a drop of greatness in every man". These enterprises portray one thing: they are able to define the orientation of their interest through their advert slogan. How do an individual define the orientation of his business enterprise? A question you may ask.

- The book, the Holy bible, recognizes the essence of defining purposes associated with business activities; "Write your vision; make it plain so that people may run through it". Therefore, defining the dynamics of business involves the basic recognition of vision and mission statements. In other worlds, making plain by writing explicating the vision and mission statements defines the business kind in terms of target audience reach production, distribution, publicity, profitability, comsumability of product, and other intentions. By identifying with the vision and mission statements, an individual is said to witness a face-lift as in them lie aims, objectives, goals, creed, policies, rules and regulations which are the most primary fact associated with business success.

- To demonstrate the power of vision and mission statements, let us consider this instance. This instance will demystify some of the business associated facts. A certain individual in the middle of a very dark night was about setting out to his abode from a very distant location without a car and no money for transport. However, he had an electrically powered touch light which he used all through the journey to his residence. Note certain assertions:

(a) "...in the middle of a very dark night..."

(b) "...setting out to his abode from a very distant location without a car and no money for transport."

(c) "...electrically powered touch light..."

(d) "...without a car and no money..."

In the light of business focus, "in the middle of a very dark night" can be interpreted as the yet – to – be – gathered bits and pieces of defining the orientation of business. "setting out to his abode from a very distant location without a car and no money for transport" means writing plain the vision and mission statement leading to success attainment without necessarily being spoon-feed by financially opulent individuals for succor and/or "fish-fed" by experienced business consultants to write on the concerned individual's behalf the vision and mission statements of the his or her business. "electrically powered touch light" simply means the guiding mission and vision statements.

On the other hand, imagine a situation where an individual decides not to switch off his or her electrically powered torchlight and walk home in the middle of that very dark night to his abode from the distant location. Do you think such an individual will make it to his abode? What do you may likely happen on his way home? Don't you think he is treading on the part of absolute obscurity a pointer of ambiguity, a haphazard and not- the- way-home route?

In reality, this is what primarily widens thegap between mega successful businesses giants and the (seemingly) not-growing business "dwarfs".Successful business people take as paramount (for starters) the essence of appreciating the statements of their mission and vision, the guide lights to the success experienced in their business. Unequivocally, they have been able to demonstrate a fact: vision statement gives a practical guide on the right approach to the mission statement. In other words, they act on the principle that states: acting on the stated vision through mission, unveiled by the mission statement is a key used in driving the vehicle of any business to the destination of anticipated success. On the other side of the coin, the (seemingly) not-growing business "dwarfs" experience unrelenting setbacks in their business because of not-properly-structured and the followed mission and vision statements. To an extent, this is the reason people fail in businesses: treading the part of ambiguity (Obscurity) instead of constructing their intended business specifics (mission and vision statements).

If you are passionate about something and you intend making is a source of livelihood, then, you are advised to make it a business success by first creating its vision and mission, in the form of statements-a product of your strategy. Also, if you are literate enough, that is, having the ability not only to read and write, but learn and be teachable, then, you can write out your vision (what you want to do with you are passionate about actualizing your vision).

What's next after the mission and vision statements must have been properly structured (written down)? A question you may want to ask. Of course, acquiring knowledge or knowing the intricacies surrounding the uniqueness of what you are about engaging in because paramount. Simply, the acquisition of knowledge is the next step, a follow-up of your constructed vision and mission statements, a subsequent and one of the not-do-without to defining the orientation of your meant-to-be successful business.

Chapter Three
Knowledge Acquisition

William Shakespeare once said: "If you are not informed, you are deformed". Francis Bacon, in paraphrased terms remarked: "Knowledge is power". Interestingly, these inspiring quotes are loosely the motto of successful business men and women. The reverse is the case for the majority; the not-growing business "dwarfs". The Holy bible, in one of its records, states: "My people perish for lack of knowledge". Precisely, people in this category, owing to limited know-how of their businesses, lack the impetus to make it successful. Consequently, their businesses crumble, despite the properly written-down vision and mission statements. Why the imbalance? What can be explained of those who are well informed about the business they are in but failed afterwards? Is knowledge acquisition just enough to succeed the most fundamental fact associated with business success? Questions are pleading to be answered!

Going back to the previous instance given, it was not enough for the individual to not only have the torchlight with him and visualize in his mind the right route to take, leading to his abode but also demonstrating what has already been visualized. In a similar fashion, knowledge acquisition, when demonstrated, an aid to an effective and worth executing mission statement, is truly a next-step criterion which is tantamount to success accomplishment. How?

Reviewing the words of William Shakespeare and Francis Bacon, there is a need for modification of the terms stated because being informed or knowledgeable about something (a particular kind of business, say) without necessary putting to effect certain efficacies of the information or knowledge gained is as good as a wild goose chase. In fact, it will stagnate certain situations (businesses) and no success will be recorded. Therefore, modifying respectively the words of William Shakespeare and Francis Bacon, we see that:

(a) "If you are not acting on what you are informed (about), you are deformed". Being informed and not acting on the informed is the same as being uninformed which is tantamount to deformity.

(b) "The action of knowledge is power". Without necessarily applying acquired knowledge, there is an obvious stagnation that will eventually become wasted. How can knowledge associated with business success be best acted on?

*There are three basic steps to acquiring knowledge related to business which are inevitably essential to business success.

(1) Studying up-to-date business materials as unveiled in books, articles and media-disseminated messages.

(2) Development of related abilities.

(3) Thirst for inspiration that breathe ingenuity and intuition.

<u>(1) Studying up - to – date business materials as unveiled in books, articles (or journals) in books, articles (or journals) and media disseminated messages.</u>

- Alerting the mind's level of information consciousness is a knowledge acquisition psyche possessed by successful business individuals. Paying the necessary dues by pains talking buying A-class business materials such as books, articles or journals through subscription or by outright purchased and subsequently studying them are facts & secretly upheld by successful business giants. Also, ardent followership of media – communicated messages, such as business seminars, workshops, symposiums, inaugural lectures and forums are associated with them. Successful business men and women get to plan; put to practice and appreciate obviously stated merits and density of practicable methodologies associated with their business.

- On the other hand, apparently not – growing business "dwarfs" are believed to be stuck to what they know. Hence, they rarely crave for up – to – date business information, the reason for their dwarfism of their business. To them, they believe in the knowledge possessed will project their businesses to the success level only to discovers resultant drastic decline.

2. <u>Development of relational abilities.</u>

The saying "no man is an island" is undoubtedly true. It is not just sufficient to study up – to – date business materials and media-disseminated messages. It involves the ability to relate with people who are successful in the same business area (preferably more experienced); getting to know the path they took to attain the present success state of their businesses – lessons learnt from their experiences, that is, their weaknesses and strengths, their orchestrated strategies; location, consumer reach, economy, ergonomics and so on. More importantly, they learn from experienced successful business giants the ability to carry along other people involved (team- playing strategy); knowing how to adopt a business synergy (win – win plan). Thomas Edison, Henry Ford and Dale Carnegie are typical examples of individuals who, though their relational skills, achieved mind – blowing exploits in their respective electro – mechanical, automobile and industrial enterprises. No doubt, some people have natural relational abilities while others do not.

Nonetheless, successful business men and women, whether possessing natural relational ability or in the process of developing such a skill see it as business success inevitable.

- On the contrary, business 'dwarfs' are relationally dis – enable; lack the power of relational ability to thoroughly 'hit' the success point in their business. A typical example is Dennis Rodman, a one – time famous basketball player. As good as he was, his relational ability was limited to the court; he fail to realize that the relating with people transcends the court. Dennis had a myopic idea of what the game was all about; the beauty of the game has its complexion completely favoring the athlete who depicts a relational attitude not only with his team mates in the court but outside its vicinity. How successful is he? Today, he is only popular amongst followers, fans and supporters of Basketball (Compare him with the likes of Michael Jordan, 'Magic' Johnson and other great basketball players who through the effective used their relational powers, are today's celebrated success in the game and business of basketball). Arguably, One quality that most (apparently) not – growing business 'dwarfs' possess is the limiting "I – know- it- all' mentality.

3. Thirst for inspiration that breathe ingenuity and intuition

- When all knowledge proves abortive or impracticable, what would you do? This question has over the years been answered by history's recognized men and women of importance. For instance, store jobs of apple computers through the genius of Steve Wosniak, attained groundbreaking business success by acting on the inspiration craved for, as unveiled by his intuitiveness, when all seem to experience upside – down results. The digit code, made apple computers one of the world's most successful computer giants. Thomas Edison, an individual who ahs three months of formal education, the highest inventive person ever (1, 093 patents to his credits), used the power of inspiration translated in institution he used to invent the electric bulb (after many failed attempts) and the ingenuity of his subsequent inventions.

Depending on what you are convinced about, inspiration may be gotten through (fervent) prayers, appreciating the essence of nature, being in an isolated or a solitary place or by meditation. Whether you believe in the power of inspiration or not it works.

Chapter Four

Keeping a Positive Attitude

- No doubt, our thoughts control or guide our actions. Therefore, keeping a positive attitude is a driving force towards reaching an anticipated business success. However, being equipped with knowledge exposes people to certain developments that dissuade them from proceeding or treading the path leading to success in their businesses. Nonetheless, successful business men and women see the attitude of taking a positive stance, no matter the discouragement. In fact, this mindset is an 'I – am – present' entity associated with business giants experiencing Mega success.

- The reverse is the case to most business dwarfs. Instead of maintain a positive psyche, they are easily influenced by discouraging information they acquire. Hence, they find themselves between the devil and deep blue sea; stagnated but are forced to withdraw from the proposed journey to business success.

- Some of us think this thought is limited to human psychology. No, on the contrary! The same principle applies. This has been the ever – guiding principle successful business individuals have over the years held on to, distinguishing their success from limited progress attained by business "dwarfs".

- Keeping a positive attitude is like the individual who decides to go home, no matter what. Otherwise, he won't be able to see himself home. No thanks to his decision! If undecided, he won't make it home, even though he is provided with a car and money for transport

- Interestingly, one of the major benefits of keeping a positive attitude is the longevity in business. Perhaps, this is one of the reasons successful business men and women are positive – minded, irrespective of imminent challenges proving hard nut to crack to surmount. By being positive, they know how successful they would become and generations to come will live to experience and benefit from their land mark achievements.

- Ford Motors, one of America's leading automobile enterprises, at a point, experienced drastic business setbacks. Nevertheless, the visionary leadership of Henry Ford, whose gaze explained "Keeping a positive attitude", decided to be compromising to the no-profit situation and limited turn-overs realized from sales of products. Specially "looking" at the future, he remained simply indefatigable. After all said and done, the almost-dying Ford Motors was resuscitated! What is Ford Motors today? One of America's leading automobile business with over a multi-million-dollar success. You and I can see the beauty of most ford cars, at least. This feat is made is made possible courtesy of Henry Ford's positive mindset against all odds.

- Let's don't forget that other automobile companies at the time of Ford motor's "trying" times were flourishing. Where are they today? No today! Why? Simply, they lacked the self-training to keep a positive altitude, despite biting business situations.

Chapter Five
Taking Calculated Risks.

- Have you heard the expression "life is a risk" before? Come to think of it, let's consider the truism of this statement. If you are driving, you may experience unforeseen accident that could claim your life or damage your car. If you are taking a walk, you may accidentally hit your leg against a very sharp object that may either cause profuse bleeding or an intense internal injury. Under the convenience of your living room, probably watching T.V, out of curiosity in wanting to know how interesting the programme you are viewing, you decided to turn-on the volume of the T.V set, not being informed about the presence of sanitary inspectors. A close-door neighbor of yours reported you to them that you are such a noise pollutant. There and then were they presented with an exhibit- the sound emanating from your abode. Consequently, you were arrested! In all, these point at the risky nature of life itself, in terms of day-to-day activities you and I engage in.

- If at this point, you still believe life can still be risk-free, then consider the walking attempts of a human baby. Instinctively, a crawling baby sees the need to 'graduate' from walking on a four-member support to a two-member support. Quite a lot of failed attempts it makes and sometimes, cries, gets injured, tried and sleeps at that spot of the failed walking attempts. The amazing thing is the baby's ability to never give up the spirit of being successful-being able to walk on two foots. Though it may take months and in some rare case, a year or two to perfect its two-foot walking the baby is sure of walking properly.

- In the same vein, this principle is applicable in the business circle. Though it is meant for every Tom, Dick and Harry, it is quite unfortunate that a handful of people who put to practice the meant-for-everybody use are the looked-up-to business role models. They simply cannot image themselves venturing into this act. Rather, the idea of staying put or holding onto security become paramount. No wonder they are referred to as the not-growing business "dwarfs". If you ask a typical successful man or woman the importance of risks in business, he or she will tell you this: no business has thrived without risk.

- Taking risks is a practical starter of business success. Are you surprised? As a matter of facts, risks mark the emergence of maturity, taking responsibility of every outcome of business actions taken (this will be explained in chapter six). Really, taking risks in business to achieve results is like you given a holder of over seventy keys from which only the right key must be appropriately chosen to unlock a door. To succeed in business, taking a risk is very important.

- Fortunately, some people take the risk and hit mega success, all at once while others take the same risk only to fail drastically far below the standard they were. Nonetheless, that doesn't change the fact that taking risk is one of the facts associated with business success.

- Like the individual whose journey was set but had no car and money for transport, the risk can be depicted if he decides to tread the path he knows very well in the middle of the very-dark night to his place of residence without wishing he had a car or money. Similarly taking calculated risks is a relatively safe approach to reaching the destination-success. The ability to take computed risks rests in the appreciation of chapters 1, 2 and 3, in practical terms (Compare what becomes of the individual treading on the path he doesn't know).

- In what situation is the phrase "taking calculated risks" best appreciated? Note: "leap before you look" is the motto of successful business giants.

Chapter Six

Minimizing Losses and Maximizing Profits.

- Business acumen is the intelligence to demonstrate the ability of prioritizing maximum profits and limiting losses, irrespective of the nature of business. To an extent, business acumen is a product of knowledge gained by reading business related materials (books articles magazines), empirical expeditions (attending seminars, workshops symposiums and inaugural lectures on business matters), relating and working with people in business and more importantly, taking calculated risks. It is in the calculated risk because acumen is made potent lessons learnt from taking computed risks enables successful business men and women maximize profit at relatively cheap costs. They know that maximizing profit and minimizing loss are a follow-up to the embarked-upon calculated risk taken which explain understanding core business success.

On my way home from a friend's get-together party, I found myself in a pub area where a MAFIA- related movie was being viewed by a host of customers. Although I did not ask of the movie title, I knew this was a typical MAFIA movie. Though the storylines were fabricated, the statements heard, in this day, are typical of the business world. The statements captured were conversations between two MAFIANs, an experienced, physically old MAFIAN and a naïve, just-initiated young MAFIAN, about twenty years of age who were engaged in tete-a-tete.

Read the following conversations carefully.

Young MAFIAN: This is the greatest day of my life. I'm happy being in this click.

Old MAFIAN: Congratulations! This is a signal of challenges to come.

Young MAFIAN: What da f**k you mean?!

Old MAFIAN: Let me ask you a question.

Young MAFIAN: Go ahead, old fox!

Old MAFIAN: Do you want to know the secrets of United States?

Young MAFIAN: I'm just 24; I'm too young to answer such a question.

*Old MAFIAN: It's money! Get that into your thick skull, fool!

The asterisk sign is our concern.

- In a sense, it will be right to assert the secret of United States' success in business is made evident courtesy of mind-blowing monetary returns from various ventures profit. Ted Turner of the CNN, Steve Jobs of Apple computers, Bill gates of Microsoft Inc., Richard Bradson of Virgin Atlantic, Mr. Ben of the Bengi (o) sophy Initiative are typical instances of people who are good at prioritizing maximized profits and limiting losses. This is what the not-growing business "dwarfs" are deficient of.

What happens if huge losses set in and maximum profits are realized? A pertinent question! This takes us to the next chapter.

Chapter Seven
Taking Responsibility For Business Actions.

- A major test of maturity in business is measured in the ability to take responsibility for outcomes of any business actions. Taking responsibility for business decisions is business circles.

- However, taking full responsibility for business actions entails having colleagues who are not only honest, dedicated, intelligent, submissive focused but are willingly to co-operate with their superiors to put the business in perspective. Otherwise, how would you want to accept the blame for or certain flaws in business were other co-workers are somewhat 'deficient' of the qualities? In simple terms, it is not easy taking such a responsibility. Rather, blaming the seen-as-dishonest, not-dedicated, not-intelligence, not-submissive, not-focus or non-cooperative colleagues becomes the other of the day. This is what differentiates success business people from business "dwarfs".

- At this junction, taking responsibility for business action are meant for success craving business people who are (or aspiring to be) strategically 'tied' to different leading business roles. In the making of an entrepreneur, investor Chief Executive Officer, Managing Director or General Manger, certain outcomes of business decisions, low or high turnover rates, profits or losses, surplus or deficit account reconciliation should be the responsibility of the would -be successful business man and woman rather than taking excuses, blaming others for negative imbalances or being self – centered in terms of taking credits for positive business returns. Instead, through a practicable win – win strategy in terms of relational abilities, business success can be fostered accepting responsibilities for good or bad business results and improving on tem or correcting them via co -operation with other team players.

- At what pinnacle of business should one aim at experience the benefits of taking responsibility for business actions?

Chapter Eight

Being Investment Minded

- This is the zenith of business success. It is a mindset residing in the lives of individuals who are experiencing and who want to experience mega business success; set the pace for others to follow, trail blazer in the endeavours they engage themselves and role models for prospective business men and women.

- The Bill Gates, Ted Turners, Stave jobs, Michael Dells, Henry Fords of this world are role models, trailblazers, pacesetters, second – to none and are unparallel in their various business enterprises. These feats are made possible by being investment minded. They are all investors! Employee, self – employer, business owner and investor attachments; the one who experience mega success how?

- Let us take a brief look at previous business attachments; self employed, business owner and employee.

  a). Self – employed: This category is a business attachment where business is dependent on the individual's continued striving and dies if the individual is no more. In fact, this attachment demands the more diligence and attention than any other. Success is limited in terms of profits and losses.

b). Business owner: This is a business attachment where success is strictly dependent on the collective efforts of the co -workers of the establishment owned by a particular person. Profit and losses go beyond the owners bounds. It can be willed to the next – of – kin or any family members.

c). Employee: This business attachment has its business success dependent on the amount of salary paid. In other words, success is salary-based. Here, job security is arguably secured. This category is seen as financially risk – free attachment. In all, taxes are paid by all the mentioned attachments (the self – employed plays most of the taxes).

- The investor's success is dependent on net return for every investment made. Hence, the investor pays low tones, is likely to be debt – free, gets richer and makes money do the working without interfering with privacy. Successful business giants know that experiencing mega success (being wealthy, say can never be achieved while working for someone.

- In a nutshell, being investment minded is practically an appreciation of defining the orientation of business, knowledge acquisition, keeping a positive mindset, taking calculated risks, maximizing profits and minimizing losses and taking responsibility for business actions.

- Calvin Coolidge, a one – time U.S. president, once said; 'America's business is businesses. Like the American dream, 'you can be anything that you want to be', you can be the business success you are as a business man or woman by considering and demonstrating these irrefutable facts.

Points to Note

1. For the successful business man or woman, instead of following the 'look before you leap' philosophy 'leap properly before you' is his or her slogan (taking calculated risks).

2 Being positive minded involves a test of one's level of determination, focus, persistence and diligence.

3. Without the written mission and vision statements, there is no business success.

Humanities

F-R-I-E-N-D-S-H-I-P: The Meaning

"Show me your friends and I will tell you who you are". This adage is undoubtedly true and used as major criterion to ascertain one's personality. In other words, an individual is known by the company he (or she) keeps. As a matter of fact, one of the means to determining the state of an individual today and in future is the friends he (or she) keeps. What kind of company do you keep?

Many people make friends, nearly on a regular basis for various purposes-commitments, encouragement, intelligence (information), intimacy and so on. Some find information but no encouragement, intimacy but absence of commitment. The list is endless! Depending on motive, friendship goes a long way in positively or negatively influencing the character of one's person. At this point, the questions 'is there a true friend and what are the qualities that would make one believe true friendship exist?' become a focus.

Consider a building. It has the obviously not seen foundation, entrance and exit points (doors and gates, for instance), louvers, concrete beams and other facilities instrumental for its completion. Imagine some of the components were absent. What do you think will happen to the building? The same goes for true friendship. When the qualities that constitute true friendship are absent, your guess is as good as mine what happens to friendship. What is true friendship and what qualities make friendship true? Questions want answers!

Mr. Ben

Introduction

F-R-I-E-N-D-S-H-I-P: The Meaning

F-R-I-E-N-D-S-H-I-P: *The Meaning* is a piece that cuts across all ages from the growing years of youthfulness to the stable years of adulthood. It also a model for organizations to attain certain stated agendas.

The title, 'Who Are Your Friends?' explains the ten ideal qualities of friendship and by implication, enables individuals be on a look-out for them as criteria for true friendship. It is applicable to organizations who crave for effective and strategic networks with other outfits for the purpose of benefits. Simply, the literary recognition applies to individuals who are in various relationships, married and corporate organizations.

The ten ideal qualities are the true qualities of friendship. They are simply unveiled in their spell-outs! How? In the first place, what is true friendship? True friendship is a foundation which is being built on by the following components: reliability, intimacy, encouragement, 'noticeability', devotion, support, happiness, information and information. The foundation which true friendship is based on is in itself made profound.

Therefore, the qualities of true friendship are unveiled in the alphabets F-R-I-E-N-D-S-H-I-P, that is,

F-Foundation

R-Reliability

I-Intimacy

E-Encouragement

N-'Noticeability'

D-Devotion/Dedication

S-Support

H-Happiness

I-Information (and)

P-Profundity

The chart below represents the presence of the qualities

Not Drawn To Scale

P

In a clockwise direction, from the arrow tending towards the north to the arrow tending towards south, are arrows representing the qualities; foundation, reliability, intimacy, encouragement, 'noticeability', devotion/dedication, support, happiness, information, profundity. Theoretically, the separations among the arrows representing the qualities are 'must-be-outstanding' interests which equally depict friendship qualities. Here, the reference point, P, is the link or friendship existing between two individuals, either in a relationship or married, two organizations or amongst individuals or organizations.

Practically, however, they are models which ought to be followed continually by individuals and organizations to ensure respective attainments of anticipated gains. In another vein, individuals and organizations can see the models as collectively a plane mirror reflecting who they ought to be (relational beings and entities) as they behold the qualities that constitute the mirror (and in that light, acting them out using the principle: what you say about yourself as you behold the glass of a mirror is what you reflect in your actions outside the mirror's territory).

Interestingly, each quality represents each chapter (as seen under the Table of Contents section). Therefore, the identity, 'Who Are Your Friends?' is a succinct ten-chapter write-up which focuses on each of the qualities using buildings, real-life stories, events and experiences as case studies. Why not flip this page?

Chapter One

Foundation

What can a righteous man do when the foundation of a building is destroyed? The Bible

The foundation of a building determines its orientation-a bungalow, duplex, two-storey building or a skyscraper. In other words, the foundation determines the kind of structure to be erected. Technically, if it is erected on a sandy foundation, the structure will with time collapse and be in ruins. On the other hand, erecting a building on concrete (or rocky) foundation will stand for all ages, irrespective of prevailing physical constraints like poor conditions of weather.

Similarly, friendship existing between and amongst individuals and organizations are defined primarily by the foundation laid. The foundation of any form of friendship existing between and amongst individuals and organizations determines the longevity of 'bonding', strength of friendship, attainment of projected aspirations via the created friendship link, level of co-operation and define the authenticity of such relationship.

Some individuals venture into friendships (commonly referred to as relationships) with others implicitly on the bases of money, sex intelligence, certain material gains and so on. Interestingly, they discover they realistically crave for the qualities which are eminent for healthy relationships. However, owing to the nature of foundation laid, their relationships hit the rock; similar to a man who laid the foundation of his building on a sandy soil!

By observation, most outfits or recognized organizations who establish friendship link (partnership) with other establishments on the basis of strictly development (for instance) discover other built-in qualities. Conversely, some setbacks organizations face are due to the not-followed essential qualities as build-ups to the laid foundation (basis of relationship in the form of partnership) as reflected in non-synergic eventuality.

At this juncture, we will consider the following terms:

1) Longevity of 'bonding'
2) Strength of friendship
3) Attainment of projected aspirations via created friendship links
4) Level of co-operation
5) Defined authenticity of friendship

Longevity of 'Bonding'

Here, 'bonding' refers to the friendship linking existing between individuals of the same sex, opposite sex (in a relationship), who are married and between/among organizations. Hence, we will consider the following:

a) Individuals who are of the same sex
b) Individuals who are of opposite sex
c) Individuals who are married
d) Between/Among organizations

a) <u>Individuals who are of the same sex</u>

The foundation on which friendship is established determines the length of friendship. Individuals make friends with their peers from childhood, youth and adulthood. Arguably, depending on distance, childhood relationships or friendships between individuals express the highest longevity of bonding. Thanks to modern technologies like the internet that provides a platform to reach out to friends, irrespective of location. The issue of distance is therefore not necessarily a topic for discussion. The older the friendship, the higher the expressed longevity of bonding.

Another period where individuals make friends is during youth. Many individuals lay the foundation of friendship on the recognition of money, sex and other trivial interests. Relatively, a number of them lay the basis of their friendship on a 'rocky' recognition. In fact, individuals whose foundations are based on trivial interests are compared to people who set or erect their houses on sandy platforms! No wonder it is said: 'in youth we learn, in age we understand'.

Finally, as adults, people make friendship. At this level, it is maturity that counts. Such a foundation should be based on understanding. Otherwise, it will yield a wild goose chase, akin to the tragic outcomes of when youths make friends on trivial bases.

Consider the following stories

Steven Gat and Frank Lam are said to have been friends since childhood. Over the years, they built the foundation of their relationship with other qualities, complementing each other in terms of 'making amends' their respective shortcomings. If Frank is intelligent (informative) and but really reliable and Steve is reliable but not informative, there is a symbiotic or mutual reconciliation of the obvious flaws (not being reliable and uninformed) through the use of their strengths (intelligence and reliability).

Lisa and Lucy became friends just after graduating from the same university. At first, both of them seemed compatible but were really not depicting their behaviours. As time progressed, Lisa discovered Lucy's shortcomings; she was unreliable, not-supporting and unintelligent. On the other hand, Lucy discovered that there is no compatibility between her and Lisa because she was not the happy type. In no time, they soon parted ways. A decade after their not being together, Lisa now understands and advises youngsters to search for outstanding qualities and make amends obviously seen shortcomings of those they intend making as friends.

Richards, a middle-aged man, has been working as a system analyst for two decades. He was later transferred to another Information Technology firm to work with a fellow IT guru, Jones. They soon became friends. Though they had their good and ugly qualities, Richards and Jones had established a level of understanding between each other in order not to put in disarray projects committed to them.

b) Individuals who are of the opposite sex

In modern times, it is almost rampant the reasons individuals venture into relationships (typical boyfriend-girlfriend relationships); money and sex. At this point, I would like to ask you a question: what happens if you built your foundation of your house on a sandy ground after a while. The right answer given to the question is an analogy to what happens to individuals who engage in relationships for the purpose of money and sex. However, there are individuals, though very few in numbers, who would take their time to build their relationships on rocky basis.

Consider this story

Stacie, a dashing young lady, 'fell in love' with Kelvin, a well-to-do gentleman. Kelvin's possessed wealth fascinated Stacie that she believed hook, line and sinker Kelvin was her man. Consequently, she gave herself to him; one thing led to the other and they got engaged. Unknown to her, Kelvin went into the union with her for the purpose of just 'using' and 'dumping' her (which he succeeded in accomplishing). Before long, the union which she thought would lead to a blissful life-long affair, considering her interest in Kelvin's wealth, was jeopardized as he realized his motive of sexually gratifying himself through her.

On what foundation is your relationship built?

c) Individuals who are married

In the first place, why did you marry him or her? Is it because of his money, looks or sexual prowess or her beauty, financial and social status or aura of intelligence? The answers depict the increasing divorce rates, estranged situations and broken homes observed in our present world. Of course, no thanks to the non-concrete ('unrocky') foundation laid. The earlier we realize that the foundation for a life-long marital friendship has to be indefatigable, the better our families and homes will be.

d) Between/Among Organizations

As CEO or Managing Director of a particular outfit (X, say), why would you establish a partnership identity with another associated establishment? Is it for the purpose of information alone? Or do you want to exploit its capital strength to maximize profit at the expense of the associated outfit? Ponder on these assertions:

The world's known companies or establishments excel in their responsibilities and services to humanity because of their built-on foundational partnership with other associates. Interestingly, their partnerships lived through the years and stood the test of time. The question you may want to ask is: 'what is the foundation itself?'

Longevity of bonding is dependent on the time exercised to 'perfect' the compatibility of friendship existing between or amongst individuals who are of the same sex, opposite sex and organizations based on foundation.

Strength of Friendship

The strength of friendship is just like asserting the strength of bonding because friendship is in itself a bond. Certainly, the strength of friendship is determined by the nature of foundation. This affects the attainment of projected aspirations via created friendship links, level of co-operation and defined authenticity of friendship. The subsequent build-up qualities are an appreciation of the 'true' strength of friendship…

Chapter Two

Reliability

You wouldn't know the worth of the word 'reliability' till situations demands of it Unknown

This is another salient quality of true friendship. Literally, reliability means ability to be relied on. In other words, reliability is a quality of friendship which pin-points at individuals who are in relationships with the same or opposite sex, married and organizations to be relied on, irrespective of circumstance. Reliability is basically friendship's quality to exhibit consistency in character.

It is a build-up to the laid foundation which establishes the quality of friendship. After the foundation of a building, a German floor or concrete is put in place to ensure the building process starts.

Have you ever wondered why influential peoples of the world entrust their wealth, resources and other material recognition to individuals, banks and other establishments, despite the presence of scam issues, financial impropriety and the economically unfriendly down-turn? Why would a man entrust in his wife's care his most treasured possession, believe in what she says without a pinch of salt, be away for a while without 'touching' her and comes back to say : 'you are such a faithful woman'? What would make someone let his girlfriend (lover) spend the night with you, knowing that you would not 'do anything with her'?

In a way, reliability is synonymous to dependability. This quality makes a soldier in the presence of his colleagues launch fierce attacks on enemy soldiers without doubting in his mind his colleagues behind him. It is the same virtue that enables you invest in a company and (possibly) entrust your possession for years, even if you hear speculations of attempted siphoning.

Come to think of it, if you are reliable, definitely, you can be trusted? Read the instance below:

Stan, a gentleman from the West Indies, has a fiancée, Micky, a beautiful-looking damsel from South Africa. Stan works with a prestigious construction company in Antigua but when less busy, he journeys to South Africa to spend quality time with his beautiful Micky. Inspite of hovering speculations about her 'playing around' with men coming from his South Africa-based friends, he has no iota of doubt about Micky's fidelity as he frequently 'meets' her without using any form of caution during his stay with her.

You do have friends; quite a number of them. Don't you? Amongst them, there is a particular individual you see as your 'best friend'. In the first place, what really made him or her your 'best friend'; sex, money or material gains? You discover that most of the friends you have cannot necessarily be confided in: It's only him! It's only her! You can completely confide in him or her certain personal issues dear to you. Put simply, your 'best friend' is someone you can trust or confide in-he or she is reliable. How did your 'best friend' attain this feat?

Reliability is sine qua non to an organization's effective network strategy. It is saying that no man is an island. In a way, no existing corporate entity can completely attain its anticipation without the lucid involvement of other associates or corporate bodies. This takes reliability to do that. Afterall, what would make a company to 'dangerously' stick out its neck to embark on a particular business function with another?

The answer is simple: reliability is certainly brought about by scaling through time-taken tests with the ability to withstand pressures arising and proven with results. Here, tests refer to individuals' or organizations' stance and pressures refer to temptation, frustration and other associated financial and material vices that question the stance of individuals or organizations.

Chapter Three

Intimacy

How do you want to know who really i am if you are not close to me? Anonymous

Undoubtedly, a vivid quality of friendship is intimacy. Intimacy is a quality that succeeds reliability. Think of it, if someone sees you as being reliable, don't you see the possibility of an existing intimate relationship?

It is a term given to closeness of acquaintance, in terms of familiarity of character, sexuality, temperament, aspiration and a sense of purpose. Intimacy is simply establishing closeness or a degree of relationship between amongst individuals and organizations.

If you are a bible-believing Christian, you would realize in the New Testament that John was very close to Jesus Christ. Hence, there was an established degree of intimacy; a close relationship existed between them. Obviously, John was dependable, that is, reliable and Jesus entrusted His entire family in his care at the point of his death (on the cross of cavalry). This was possible because of an established intimacy.

Intimacy goes a long way in determining the longevity of relationship existing between individuals and married people. Divorce cases, estranged status and demise that are eminent result from lack of intimacy.

Henry, a Canadian farmer, was born in 1899. Canada's Ann was born in 1904. In 1921, Henry got married to Ann. In 2001, their union was the oldest marriage the world has ever known, thanks to the presence of intimacy. Without this quality, such lifelong marriage would be truncated as life's thick and thin jeopardizes marital togetherness.

Intimacy creates the nearness of individuals in relationships, marriages and organizations. With intimacy, individuals and organizations get to know each other and consequently define salient issues that connect them.

Joan was accused of attempted murder and detained afterwards. Michelle, a close of her's, at the court of law, pin-pointed at how their closeness positively affected her life, changed her from a die-hard gangster to a willing-to-die- for-man martyr. She gave instances and evidences depicting Joan's behaviour that the judge was left with no other choice than to adjourn the case by a forthnight. After several deliberations, the judge's verdict went in favour of the accused Joan. If not for the level of intimacy existing between Joan and Michelle, what do you think would likely be Joan's fate, knowing that the 'set-up' stage was well planned out?

Intimacy is a factor responsible for investments made towards the continued sustainability of various organizations. For instance, individuals, corporate bodies with international recognition 'put' their confidence (wealth) as investment in the money-spinning oil business, on the grounds of trade relations, professional cordiality and association with major players in the oil world. This is simply an appreciation of intimacy.

Intimacy is a sureness asserting the bond of friendship through exerted closeness (in-depth inquiry and discovery into certain intricacies of man-sexuality, temperament and sense of purpose) and manifested as knowledge-defined means of mutual accomplishment by individuals and organizations.

Chapter Four

Encouragement

Discouragement brings about failure but encouragement brings about success... Forest Gump (Paraphrased)

The term 'encouragement' is important for the continued of any aspect of man's recognition, especially friendship. Encouragement is a household name which not only merits consideration but cuts across all forms of relationships existing between individuals and organizations. Without encouragement, friendship will lose its efficacy.

The analysis explains its dynamics. Encouragement means the attainment of entrusted courage. In other words, it is a word which is made realizable when courage is entrusted in the hands of concerned individuals to 'keep' and give it back as the demonstration of character when handling issues.

Great men and women who attained breath-taking successes have unequivocally learned to lean strongly on the word 'encouragement'. As a matter of fact, the success behind men who had made landmarks in history came from the words of encouragement by their friends. Inspite of leaving school at a period least expected, Bill Gates, CEO of Microsoft Inc., was encouraged by his wife and friend and Co-founder of Microsoft Inc., Paul Allen, to demonstrate the character of projected accomplishment (computer programs such as the Microsoft office equipment), despite opposition from every Tom, Dick and Harry, connected with his affairs at the time, by entrusting the attained words of courage in his possession.

If you are in a relationship or married, how well do you encourage your spouse to be who he or she ought or want to be? Encouragement brings out mutual appreciation of each other's effort thereby giving the relationship or marriage a meaning. Contrary to what has been stated, lack of encouragement, which is tantamount to discouragement, widens communication gap; thereby permitting concerned spouses to seek for solace elsewhere which is a starter of an eventual demise or divorce.

In friendship, irrespective of religion, it is advised that people should encourage each other because life's journeys are full of challenges, not willing to allow easy accomplishment of aspirations. This is an indispensable quality of friendship. Encouragement is like a catalyst that defines the strength of friendship.

If you are in the sciences, you would appreciate this instance: The food taken in the body must be acted on by enzymes (otherwise known as organic catalyst) before complete digestion and other bio-chemical activities can take place in the human body. They determine the rate at which food intakes are absorbed. Similarly, encouragement is an emotional or a mental catalyst that determines the strength of friendship in terms of goal accomplishment through demonstrated character. The 'weaker' the level of encouragement, the less likely man will attain his expectations.

In fact, it is fascinating to know that individuals do not necessarily get to propel themselves towards becoming who they are except for the infallible words of encouragement from their friends. This statement has everything to do with me: Growing up, I was a one-way person-one who believes that everything in life gravitates towards you provided you focus on your academics. I read books, studied for at least eight hours daily and worked on some weird calculations. Though I had a flair for creative writing, I was overwhelmed by the euphoria of high grades I obtained while in high school. However, after words of re-orientation by friends on the need to reaching out to give my writing skill a developmental approach, I moved in this light. Here I am (now) shaking my world for good! I do not mean you do the same. Afterall, what worked for me may not really work for you! Know yourself! All I am saying is: your evaluation of what people have encouraged you about (perhaps, your potentials) to work on is what matters.

Not only people who are in relationships or married need encouragement, companies, establishments and other corporate interests need a great deal of entrusted courage to depict competence to climb the ladder of resuscitation of service rather than debasing them to the abyss of irrevocable financial insolvency, despite the presence of prevailing storms of economic crisis.

Chapter Five
'Noticeablility'

You are like Mount Zion; a city set upon a hilltop. Who can deny seeing you? The Bible (Paraphrased)

What is hidden under the sun? Obviously nothing! 'Noticeability' is a quality associated with friendship. In the context of friendship, 'Noticeability' means the ability of the linked being noticed, seen or known by all and sundry (Notice + Ability=Ability to be Noticed='Noticeability') How?

Depending on the nature of the land, the foundation of a building determines the level of how noticed the structure would be. Given normal circumstance, the foundation of a bungalow structure is anticipated to be less noticed than a duplex building. A duplex building is expected to be less noticed than a well-structured skyscraper.

In the same vein, the kind of foundation determines how obvious or noticeable friendship existing between or amongst individuals. The height of friendship existing between or amongst individuals is a statement of 'noticeability'. The greater the height of friendship, the more noticeable it will become. The height of friendship is dependent on the nature of foundation (sex, money and love).

You have friends, don't you? If you do, how noticeable is your friendship to people around you? Have they known that you have friendly relations with him or her? The question, when answered correctly, brings to the spotlight the quality, 'noticeability'.

If you have been an avid viewer of the famous World Wrestling Entertainment (WWE), the names Shawn Michaels and Triple H are not just mega-stars but long-time friends. Their friendship became stronger through the years that the whole WWE universe is aware of this strong bond existing between them. Although they get to confront each other in the ring, a professional ambit of wrestling that both of them must submit to, they are really friends, out of the ring. This link has attracted the notice of members and viewers of WWE universe and the entire entertainment world.

True friendship acknowledges 'noticeability'. 'Noticeability' is the recognition influenced by the dynamic consequence of built foundation between or amongst individuals, attracting the attention of people or drawing the attention of observant individuals.

Chapter Six

Dedication/Devotion

<u>*A committed man is not lost in the things he has committed himself to*</u> Popular saying

Dedication or devotion is undoubtedly a mentioned quality of true friendship. Devotion is synonymous with faithfulness, discipline and transparency (sincerity). It applies to individuals and organizations. Without the influence of dedication in any relationship, such a relationship will lose its true values. Faithfulness, commitment, discipline and transparency will be buttressed to assert how applicable they are to individuals and organizations.

a) Faithfulness: This term exerts its appreciation by individuals who are in various relationships and married and organizations that seek posterity. Faithfulness is a conscious effort borne out of heartfelt decisions, compelled by a force of strong conviction and manifested as 'stickability' to a particular cause or entity.

If you are in a relationship, how faithful are you to your spouse? If he or she acts wrongly, would you still uphold faithfulness? Sexually, are you worth being faithful to? In money and other related matters, can you say: 'I am faithful to my spouse'? The right (personal) answers given to the asked questions will determine the real value of such relationship. The same questions apply to those who are married. The wrong answers provided practically account for observed infidelity, divorce and estranged situations and broken homes. If an individual is faithful, then such a person is committed. A committed person is therefore disciplined.

b) Discipline: A faithful person is the one who 'punishes' his or her natural or fleshy desires for the sake of accomplishing certain set goals. That's discipline! In a way, discipline is an evidence of faithfulness. No man can say 'I am devoted to something' without exercising discipline. This is because setbacks, challenging (tempting) situations are inevitable-they question the authenticity of man's devotion. Irrespective of your level of relationship, the absence of discipline amounts to nothing except you are not serious about the institution you are in. For the married, it is one of the most essential 'check and balance' precepts to truncate observed excesses, no matter the prevailing situations. Of course, a disciplined person is a transparent one. The issue of transparency is the most sought-after recognition by individuals who are married or in relationships and prospect-driven organizations.

c) Transparency: If you looked at a mirror, you will see an express image of yourself. This instance is a reflection of what many people crave for and corporate entities desire. If you are transparent (sincere) to your spouse in the relationship you are in, if you exercised the 'mirror-action', in your marriage and if an organization is equipped with the virtue of transparency in all facets of its recognition, the resultant is a statement of continued togetherness, marital bliss and progress respectively. Note: Dedication/Devotion comes with a sacrifice.

Chapter Seven

Support

We all need support in our dealings with people... Author

Support is essential for continued friendship. The quality, support, cuts across all forms of friendship; individuals who are in various relationships and marriages and organizations.

Imagine if you, as an individual or organization, were not supported by a friend, family member or associate, at one point in time, do you really think you can attain that level of recognition you presently occupy?

Come to think of it, the lion, the king of the jungle, requires the support of all other 'lesser' animals for its identity as their head.

Indeed, the partnership existing between the worlds's recognized CEO giants Bill Gates and Paul Allen have come a long way. If not for the financial succor by Paul Allen which hugely facilitated the advent of the consumer-friendly Microsoft Inc., do you see the possibility Bill Gates' growing fame and fortune? Without the support of Paul Allen, where do you think Bill Gates and Microsoft Inc. be today?

The presence of support creates the backbone of friendship. This quality is similar to the function of the vehicle's shock absorber and the human cartilage.

No matter the form of constraint, support is a defense to cushion or completely truncate the adverse effect(s) posed by physically unhealthy pressures.

Sir Isaac Newton, arguably the greatest physicist of all time, achieved profound break-throughs in science through support. It is said that 'great things starts from little beginnings'. Newton, during his youth, spent most of his time in seclusion and worked assiduously in putting on paper mathematical ideas of naturalistic philosophy. Subsequently, his friend, Edward, an astronomer, saw his works spread around his room and asked him if he minded his works being published at his expense. Newton agreed to his proposal and that was it! The book titled 'principia' set the young Isaac Newton to limelight with the support of his astronomer friend, Edward.

Martin Luther King Jr., a celebrated black human rights activist and the youngest black to receive a Nobel Laureate prize, achieved these feats with the support of his loving wife, Coretta Scott King. In marriage, the standing of a man as head is made concrete by the support of his wife. The oldest marriage in the world (as of 2001), that is, the marriage between Henry and Anna Jevas, was celebrated owing to the support of Henry's backbone, Anna, all through the years of good and bad times.

Organizations require support from others, if necessary, for continued sustainability and growth. Partnership that exists between or amongst internationally known outfits is realized through the appreciation of support. Without the International Monetary Fund playing crucial roles in reviving my apparently dying economies and known establishments of the world, they would become vague in reality.

Chapter Eight
Happiness

Don't worry, be happy… Lion King sound track excerpt

Sincerely, how do you feel when you get to know someone at prima fascie better? Happy! I guess. How would you feel when your friend or business partner does not feel happy? What would you do afterwards?

Happiness is basically the state of the mind and can be reflected by an individual and infected to others, no matter how pathetic the atmosphere may be. Happiness is a crucial quality of true friendship. Personally, imagine your relationship without happiness… Friendship flourishes when there is happiness.

If you are a sad-looking person how do you associate people with you? How are going to attract happy people? If you act in the light of dismay, how would you make friends? Have you taken your time to observe that most unhappy people hardly make friends? In fact, people do not associate with individuals who are physically sad-looking. It scares them!

People get easily attracted to individuals who can make them happy, irrespective of relationship status. This story says it all:

Cynthia Green and Audrey Reid are lovers. They have been lovers since high school. Cynthia is beautiful, intelligent, loving and charitable. Her only 'but' is her naturally non-lively type. In fact, the facial look, though generally beautiful, is dominated by a frown-looking appearance that creates unhealthy association with other people.

On the other hand, Audrey is an average-looking but very sociable person. He relates with every Tom, Dick and Harry he came in contact with. In the eyes of friends of Audrey and Cynthia, they were both seen as opposites!

At every notice of Audrey's friendly behaviour, she flares up at him in the open without minding where she is. This development continued to a point Audrey almost got fed up that he thought of a conceived 'break-up' approach.

Meanwhile, Monica, a secret admirer of Audrey, is fun to be with. She is very jovial and approachable. Because of the character she possessed, she became the cynosure of all eyes (Audrey inclusive). Although Audrey loves Cynthia, he prefers the company of Monica because of her inviting happiness disposition.

Mandy and Andrew have been married for five years and have their union blessed with two lovely children. However, Andrew's unhappy mood posses a hard nut to crack task to Mandy's approach to handling male's visitors and admirers. Andrew's unhappy look scares away his neigbours and strongly dissociates people from keeping him company. Mandy spends time seeking for friendship with her female colleagues at her place of work. Indeed, she longs for happiness.

Happiness is an expression which evidently defines the association between or amongst individuals by 'infecting' and reflecting the aura of warmth, peace and a temporal ease from disdain, excruciation, frustration and or confusion to others.

Chapter Nine
Information

If you are not informed, you are deformed William Shakespear

The above expression is true. In fact, with this mind, Francis Bacon's 'Knowledge is power' is better appreciated. The significant difference that exists between or amongst individuals, baring gender, is the quality of information possessed. From the first expression, it can be deduced that if there is information, friendship between or amongst people will not suffer setbacks.

In a relationship, either individual A or B or both must be properly have in possession information to avoid the chance of a possible demise from occurring. Here, information has to do with how to cope and establish weaknesses and strengths of the personas of individuals A and B through encouragement, discipline, sincerity and communication against fluctuating vices of social interaction. For instance, a man should be equipped with the necessary information needed for financial prosperity and growth in order to ensure stability of relationship with his spouse. Else, the risk of a possible break-up is eminent.

In the prevailing era of economic and socio-political crisis, married couples must crave passionately for quality information necessary for continued thriving and security of their marriage. At this period, a wife or husband who does not really understand the growing and changing demands of his or her spouse and home will create a discrepancy resulting in a estranged situation between the man and his wife, divorce or even a broken home (where children become the victims of the unhealthy marital circumstances).

Moreover, organizations will need up-to-date qualitative information to improve on the standard of their operations. Information is sine qua non to any establishment's growth; effective network strategy. It is always advisable for organizations to therefore seek highly informed individuals whose knowledge will speedily necessitate the advancement of their recognition (effective network strategies), irrespective of status, class or qualification.

Chapter Ten

Profundity

Love is infinite in length, width and height; in fact, in all dimensions, love is profound Anonymous

A building is complete if the essential facilities such as the louvers, exit and entrance points, roof-tops, and other materials are put in place as build-ups on its laid foundation. Afterall, what is the essence of laying a building's foundation without building on it? Can a building be said to be complete if there are no roof-tops and louvers? The foundation of a building is made complete when all the essential components necessary for its completion are all put in place.

The strength of a building's foundation determines the weight of other building materials it can bear. You do not expect the foundation of a bungalow building to carry a load equivalent to that of a skyscraper. Else, the building will be razed! Similarly, the strength of friendship is determined by the nature of foundation laid. You would not expect a friendship situation whose foundation was laid on sex to 'carry' the qualities of encouragement, support and dedication. It will be out of place to lay the foundation of friendship on money to anticipate reliability and intimacy. It will only hit the rocks!

The quality, profundity, is the definition given to the dynamics of strength of friendship, determinant of the attainment of projected aspirations via created friendship link and defined authenticity of friendship. Certainly, profundity affects friendship's longevity of 'bonding'. It is the ideal appreciation of all the qualities; intimacy, reliability, encouragement, 'noticeability', support, information, happiness and dedication/devotion on a 'particular' laid foundation. The more deep or intense the foundation of friendship is, the higher its longevity of 'bonding' and strength. By a careful deduction, the deepest or most profound friendship link exists if the foundation laid on the most concrete platform or soil; the 'particular' foundation.

The profundity of the idealized qualities is what individuals and organizations should be on a look-out for follow-ups in order to improve their relationship stances when making friends or associations (partners). The question is: 'where can I locate the most concrete foundation for me to experience the most profound friendship'?

The answer is…Infinite Love!

www.ingramcontent.com/pod-product-compliance
Lightning Source LLC
LaVergne TN
LVHW061546070526
838199LV00077B/6918